Grace In The Flames:
Discovering God's Power In Fiery Trials

Grace In The Flames:

Discovering God's Power In Fiery Trials
Douglas Scott Martin

Published By Douglas Scott Martin
2015

First Printing: 2015

ISBN 978-1-312-54823-7

Douglas Scott Martin

www.grace2overcome.com

Dedication

To my best friend, Justin Thill, for challenging me on and helping me see the light at the end of the tunnel, to my friend, Cayce Talbott, who has been pivotal in my life concerning the Grace of God, to my friends, Brian Francis Hume, Cameron Brice, Marcus Hartwig, Miles Phelps, and Rick Lindsay for all your encouragement; my Dad John Rutherford Martin for being an awesome father and man of God; my children Jordan Grace, Melody Joy and Micah Douglas just because I have the best kids in the world; my pastors, Dexer Easley, Al Brice, Thomas Beard and Scott Kirsch for all your leadership, my ex-wife Emily Martin who pushed me to write this book in the beginning, and all the neighsayers who told me I couldn't. Neener, neener.

I say, "Thank you" with a big fat sloppy wet kiss! Well, maybe without the kiss.

Table of Contents

ACKNOWLEDGEMENTS 11

CHAPTER 1: THE UNCHALLENGED VIEW 13
   AN OLD ENIGMA..13
   LOVE AND ABUSE..14
   WHY DO WE NEED TO REEVALUATE? 15

CHAPTER 2: THE GRAND OPPORTUNITY 19
   THE TOKEN PHRASE FOR LOSS 19
   WHO WAS JOB?..20
   A HEAVENLY SOAP OPERA..23
   AROUND THE THRONE OF GOD..24
   UNCOVERING A MATTER..25
   GOD AND GAMBLING 27
   NEVERTHELESS 28
   SERIOUSLY?..30

CHAPTER 3: JOB'S ACHILLES HEEL 33
   THE FACES OF FEAR..33
   LIKE A ROARING LION 35
   FAITH VS. FEAR 35

CHAPTER 4: THE GREAT WAR STRATEGIST 37
   NOW THERE WAS A DAY 37
   THE BODY OF SATAN...39
   JOB'S HOSTILE NEIGHBORS 40
   THE DEVIL'S TORNADO 47
   SATAN'S PRECISION 48

CHAPTER 5: TIME TO FACE THE MUSIC 53
   LEGALITY AND LOOPHOLES 53
   GROWING UP AND FACING THE WORLD................................55
   THE FEAR OF LOSS..57
   STRATEGY AND EFFICACY..59
   UNWAVERING DEVOTION? 60
   A NOT-SO-CELEBRATORY CELEBRATION 61

CHAPTER 6: THE SECOND WAVE 63
   NOW THERE WAS A DAY AGAIN, AGAIN 63
   WHY NO TWENTY QUESTIONS?...66

CHAPTER 7: JOB'S WIFE'S WISDOM...................................67
   TOTALLY MISUNDERSTOOD 67

THE ALMOST AUDIBLE VOICE 68
THE THING ABOUT GLACIERS 69
THE REAL VICTIM 70

CHAPTER 8: THE WICKED MOB BOSS 75
JOB AND HIS SWEARING PROBLEM 75
JOB'S "HEAVENLY PLATITUDES" 77
THE MISUNDERSTOOD MASTER 90
COUNTING IT ALL AS LOSS...91

CHAPTER 9: GOT COMPASSION?...............................93
OUR NATURAL RESPONSE 93
RESPONSE AND RESPONSIBILITY 93
CULTURAL HINDRANCES 96
DUPLICITY AND BAD DOCTRINE 97
LEGION PART 2 98

CHAPTER 10: THREE IDOL WORSHIPPERS 101
LARRY, MOE AND CURLY 101
SEVEN DAYS OF WHAT?!..103
WHAT'S IN A NAME?..105
THE SPONGE AND THE SPOUT 109
A RESURRECTION HOPE..110
WHAT GOD IS NOT...111

CHAPTER 10: LET'S TALK ABOUT IDOLATRY 115
PHARISEES BEFORE THERE WERE PHARISEES 115
WORSHIPING WORSHIP 117
TWO OPTIONS 119

CHAPTER 11: JOB'S COUNTERSUIT 121
OH, NO HE DIDN'T! 121
THE "RIGHTEOUSNESS" OF JOB 121
WHAT A TWIST! 124
JOB'S PERSONAL LIST OF ACCOLADES 125

CHAPTER 12: THE YOUNG MAVERICK 129
LOOK AT ME! LOOK AT ME! 129
FASHIONABLY LATE..130
THE GLASS GLOBE...136
USED BY GOD?..137

CHAPTER 13: THE GREAT DEFENDER........................139
BEING PUT IN ONE'S PLACE 139
THE PARADIGM SHIFT...139

PRIDE AND PRIDE...142
INTIMACY WITH GOD 144
WHEN IGNORANCE REALLY IS BLISS.....................................148
GOD'S SOLUTION TO THE THIRD POWER..............................151

CHAPTER 14: *OVERCOMING A JOB EXPERIENCE* **155**
WHAT NOW?...155
WRITE ANOTHER CHAPTER 157
FREEDOM IN THE FURNACE 159

CHAPTER 15: *GOD'S SUPER ABOUNDING GRACE* **161**
SERIOUSLY AND OBSESSIVELY OVER AND ABOVE....................161
INSULTING GOD'S SPIRIT AND TRAMPLING JESUS..................165
JOB AND HIS INSOLENCE 168

CHAPTER 16: *OVERCOMING HABITUAL CRISIS* **169**
MY LAST RESTART..169

CHAPTER 16: *CONCLUSION* **173**

Acknowledgements

I would like to thank my editor, Tiffany Coulter, my typing teacher in high school (I forget her name), my friends for all their input, and my family without whose help this book would never have been completed.

Thank you for your patience and guidance, your use of the editor's red pen...

Chapter 1: The Unchallenged View

An Old Enigma

The Book of Job is something of an enigma to the Church. It is one of the most controversial books in the Bible because, on some levels, it seems to contradict the rest of the Bible. It's time we take a closer look at the Book of Job.

For so long, I believe that we have accepted a view of Job's "dilemma" that has not been challenged. This pious view is void of feeling and emotion, and, on some levels, is very legalistic. It doesn't take into account the cultural setting, the time period, the character of God, the character of Satan and many other things that are crucial for finding meaning in the story. This accepted viewpoint looks at the story as just a story. It never gets to the heart of the matter.

The reality is that all of the people involved are living breathing people with feelings and faults and weaknesses, including Job. In order to move past religious tradition and to the story of grace and redemption God is showing here, we are going to look at these people through the eyes of compassion and identify with the tragedy of Job and his wife. We are going to identify with their frailties and heartache. We are going to address each person's "God View" and place it next to scripture and see how it measures up. We are going to bring Jesus Christ into the mix and the old phrase of "What Would Jesus Do?"

Lastly, we are going to take the story and apply it to today with some of the mindsets and belief systems that mold and shape the present church and her saints. Rather than holding Job up as an impossible standard and his friends as fictional characters or "archetypes" for us to try to identify, we are going to look at the Book of Job through the eyes of humanity. As we do this you will notice that while it is a different culture and time, we are faced with the same mind sets and hang-ups. Three things remain the same throughout time: God, Satan and Humanity. We are about to discover that Job's story is really our own story. Let's begin. Hold on to your hats because the ride begins a little rough.

Love And Abuse

What is so wonderful about a God who plays favorites? You know what I am talking about.

- He wills to heal some people, but He wills to afflict others.

- He wills to financially bless these faithful saints, but He wills to bring poverty and ruin to those.

- He gives abundantly to these and takes away from those.

- In some cases He even gives and then takes it right back.

- He puts sickness on some to teach them patience.

- He kills a mother with cancer and a father with leukemia so that their kids can have a powerful testimony.

- He dangles something just out of reach to get you to obey and keep you following until the bitter end.

- He does all of these things in the name of Sovereignty and we are never allowed to question it or hold God to the same standards that He has placed on us.

Now that I have you thinking (and probably a little perplexed), I will tell you that I am only quoting much of mainstream Christianity. I've known a pastor that said, "God gave me diabetes to teach me humility and to pray more." And then he would quote an isolated passage of scripture to prove his point. You know what I am talking about. (Actually, he gave himself diabetes by way of out of control eating habits and a Lazy Boy Recliner.) We've all done it at some point in our Christian walk. Maturity in God happens so much faster when we stop conforming the Word of God to fit us, and start letting God conform us to His Word.

Back to the subject at hand, there are plenty of people in the Body of Christ who believe that sickness and disease are given by God at times to teach and mature us, Yet out of the other side of their mouths they say, "God is a good God and a loving Father."

Well, which is it? Make up your mind here. The imagery I get with this is of an abusive father and husband who hits his wife and says "This is the only way you listen" and then when he calms down says, "I do it because I just love you so much!", "To hear that from an abusive father is appalling. It is ridiculous to believe that a father who physically abuses you and intentionally harms you is a good parent. Most people in their right minds would argue against it immediately. And yet, a great majority of the church believes this exact thing about God.

Let's rephrase my previous statement with God put into it. "It is ridiculous to believe that Father God Who physically abuses you and intentionally harms you with sickness, disease and death is a good Father."

I think that you can now see this is junk, but unfortunately there is a large amount of misunderstood scripture that needs to be reevaluated. God is a good God. God is a good Father. Because of this, we need to take a closer and deeper look at some major doctrines in the body of Christ that don't line up with truth.

Why do we need to reevaluate?

Well, for one thing, many people, me included, grew up with this "doctrine" and it messed them up. I remember at the age of 18 thinking that God actually hated me. Thank you, "Hellfire and Brimstone" preaching. I had known Jesus since I was three years old. I came to the conclusion, after listening to years and years of brazen "Obey God or else" preaching, that God hated me. This is shocking for some saints to even grasp, but it is an epidemic in the Body of Christ today. In 1994 at a Summer Camp in Maine, when I was 18, I went up to the evangelist after the first night's service was over and asked if he had a minute to talk. "What would you like to ask me?" he asked.

I said, "Why does God hate me?!" then I began heaving and sobbing uncontrollably. It just came out! I can still feel the intense emotions of that moment. That wasn't what I wanted to say at all, but a dam broke inside and I could hold it no longer. My heart physically hurt from the pain inside. The poor man didn't know what to do with me. After crying for a while I regained my composure and he prayed with me.

I lived so many years with such a dead feeling inside my heart because of this hidden heart issue. I had two opposing, yet coexisting doctrines inside me that caused constant torment. It says in the Word that a double minded man is unstable in all of his ways. This was definitely true for me and for the many others who struggled with tormenting thoughts.

So many people have come to the conclusion, after being indoctrinated with garbage and confusion for years, that they are not the favorite of the litter. Some people even feel unloved by God. Some people take an even more tragic step further and believe that they are hated by God. I know that pain. It is the worst kind of pain. You walk around in absolute sorrow. I used to let out these deep bitter sighs with my shoulders hunched over. I wanted to just disappear and die for years. What was the point?

I was a believer who truly believed that God hated me. It was the great paradox. I served the God who displayed the greatest love on the Cross, and yet believed that this same Loving God hated me. It doesn't seem possible, but it happens all the time with saints.

It took many long difficult years for God to penetrate my heart and bring healing. God is such a good God. He patiently and tenderly would reach out to me in love. Even though I fought His hand, He never gave up on me.

You know, if I had been taught right, if I had known the Loving God for who He was and is, I wouldn't have had to go through that long process of healing. Because of that, I am writing this to reach out to others who are in the same boat that I was in. This is for you. You can be free, and your answer lies in one of the most uncomfortable books in the Bible; the book of Job.

The Token Phrase For Loss

"The Lord gives and the Lord takes away!"

I don't know how many times I have heard this quoted right after some terrible calamity has struck someone. A mother dies with pancreatic cancer, *"The Lord gives and the Lord takes away!"*

A father of five loses his job, *"The Lord gives and the Lord takes away!"*

A teenage son dies of a drug overdose, *"The Lord gives and the Lord takes away!"*

A mother-to-be miscarries for the third time, *"The Lord gives and the Lord takes away!"*

Your neighbor's car is repossessed, *"The Lord gives and the Lord takes away!"*

A grandfather develops Alzheimer's disease, *"The Lord gives and the Lord takes away!"*

Do we even know what we are saying? This phrase is often said with a bit of pride like you just earned a Holy Merit Badge or something. It is the token phrase for loss which is a bit ironic.

I met a man once whose whole family died in their house as it burnt to the ground. He came home to find the house still smoldering. The first thing he did when he got out of the car was throw his hands up in the air knowing that his whole family died in the fire and say, "The Lord gives and the Lord takes away! Blessed be the Name of the Lord!" He thought it was a test from the Lord that he had to pass. WHAT?! I'm sure that if God wanted to teach him something that there are 1,000,000 other ways to teach it without the need to kill off his family.

Job uttered that same phrase when he lost everything. He is a man of a thousand words, yet no one ever quotes the other 992 words of his. There is a big reason for that. Job was a very bitter, fearful, prideful man and quite sarcastic with his description of the character and ways of God. We will go into those heavenly platitudes later on, but first, for those who don't know exactly who Job was, let's start at the beginning:

Who Was Job?

Job 1:1-3 (HCSB[1]) *"There was a man in the country of Uz named Job. He was a man of perfect integrity, who feared God and turned away from evil. He had seven sons and three daughters. His estate included 7,000 sheep, 3,000 camels, 500 yoke of oxen, 500 female donkeys, and a very large number of servants. Job was the greatest man among all the people of the east."*

That is quite the introduction! It says that Job lived in the land of Uz. This is not to be confused with the land of Ur where Abraham was from. Uz, not Ur. Although it does seem strange to name two cities after sounds you make when you can't think of an answer, the naming of a city in Ancient times was given a lot of thought. Ur, for instance, according to Wikipedia:

"The city's patron deity was Nanna, the Sumerian moon god, and the name of the city is in origin derived from the god's name, URIM being the classical Sumerian spelling of LAK-UNUG[1], literally 'the abode of Nanna.'"

(http://en.wikipedia.org/wiki/Ur)

I think Lakunug would have been a much better choice for the naming of a city than Ur. (Actually, my kids love going to the abode of their Nanna. She spoils them. This kind of makes you want to make your kids call their Nanna something else instead of the name of Sumeria's patron deity. Well, maybe in some cases, the name Nanna is appropriate. I'm probably digging my own grave here.)

---

[1] Holman Christian Standard Bible

The Land of Uz, however, is a bit harder to locate. Wayne Blank, in his Daily Bible Study gives us a few clues.

"The precise location of the land of Uz is uncertain, although the Bible record does provide some clues: The land may have originally been named after Uz, who was the son of Aram, and grandson of Shem (Genesis 10:23, 1 Chronicles 1:17). One of Job's friends, Eliphaz, came from Teman (Job 4:1), which is in Idumea. Uz was subject to attacks from Sabeans and Chaldeans (Job 1:15,17). It had to have fertile pastures, since Job had many thousands of animals. It had at least one major city, since Job sat at the city gate. The two most likely locations for the land of Uz is in Arabia, east of Petra (today, northwestern Saudi Arabia), or more likely, in Bashan, east of The Sea Of Galilee and south of Damascus (today, western Jordan or southern Syria)."

(Where Was Uz? Wayne Blank – The Church Of God Daily Bible Study)

It is speculated by a majority of Biblical Theologians that the Book of Job predates Moses. Chuck Smith, one of my favorite speakers, in his commentary on the Book of Job says this concerning Job's place in the Old Testament:

"So Job is the first of the books of poetry. It has been considered perhaps older than the book of Genesis. Though Genesis, of course, deals with history that predates Job, yet there is a Jobab mentioned in Genesis that is very possibly the Job of this book who lived contemporarily with Abraham. So it is possible that Job dates back as far as does Abraham, just a couple of generations away from Noah and the flood. Thus, in the book of Job, which is one of the oldest books of man's literature, the

expression of the thoughts of some of the earliest men, once writing was developed and thoughts could be recorded. We find that men from the beginning have been pretty much the same. Though our cultures have changed and times have changed from Job, yet basically the same things that were a problem to Job are the same things that become a problem to us. The same needs that Job expressed are the same needs that still exist in man today." [2]

Notice that Job's wealth was determined not just by gold but also by his livestock. Back then, livestock was as good as currency. In early cultures the bartering system was used where one person would trade something they needed less for something they needed more; i.e. a cow for a donkey, or an ox yoke for bags of feed. Abraham's wealth was also determined by his livestock. So, we get a picture of the time that Job lived in.

Let's look at some of the puzzle pieces for just a minute.

Job and Jobab could very well be the same person.

Job lived in Uz.

Uz was the grandson of Noah.

Jobab was the great great nephew of Uz.

Uz was both a city name and Shem's grandson's name.

Job, who was the wealthiest man of his time, could have lived in the land that may have been founded by his great great uncle, Uz.

It is really interesting to think about.

What about his family life?

Job 1:4-5 (HCSB) *"His sons used to have banquets, each at his house in turn. They would send an invitation to their three sisters to eat and drink with them. Whenever a round of banqueting was over, Job would send for his children and purify them, rising early in the morning to offer burnt offerings for all of them. For Job thought:*

---

[2] Through the Bible Commentary, C-2000 Series

"Perhaps my children have sinned, having cursed God in their hearts. This was Job's regular practice."

So, we see that Job had ten children who were adults with their own households. Job had already lived a successful and blessed life raising 10 children and sending them out to live their own lives. It appears that Job's children were also wealthy in that they would hold banquets on a frequent basis. Job must have been in the 40 to 60 years old range. It is not said.

An interesting side note is the author makes mention of Job attempting to keep his children pure in the eyes of the Lord. He had a thought concerning the purity of his children that would trouble him constantly, thus he kept a regular practice of purifying them and offering burnt offerings for them. The reason that this is mentioned is because it becomes a major issue in the plot of this story later on in Chapter 3.

On a side note, I'm wondering why none of them had a practice of purifying themselves or offering burnt offerings to the Lord. Job may have failed in training up his children to worship his God. This also becomes a major issue later on. Remember these two things.

A Heavenly Soap Opera

Now, let's talk about what got Job into this whole mess:

Job 1:6-9 (NASB[3]) *"Now there was a day when the sons of God came to present themselves before the Lord, and Satan also came among them. The Lord said to Satan, "From where do you come?" Then Satan answered the Lord and said, "From roaming about on the earth and walking around on it." The Lord said to Satan, "Have you considered my servant Job? For there is no one like him on the earth, a blameless and upright man, fearing God*

---

[3] New American Standard Bible

and turning away from evil." Then Satan answered
the Lord, "Does Job fear God for nothing?"

I want to look at a few things before we go further. First of all, you can't just look at this and say, "Nothing fishy here!" It says, "Now there was a day. . ." which means, it was one day among many, yet it was different from the others. How was it different? In order to figure that out, first we have to establish what was normal. There are days and then there was "a day".

This actually happens three times in the book of Job where the author says, "Now there was a day" which shows three significant turns in the story.

Around The Throne of God

Looking at this we can assume that the sons of God presenting themselves before God was the normal routine, yet on this particular day, we see something else happening in the mix. Here is an easy question. When do the angels present themselves to God? ALL THE TIME, FOREVER! That is what they do. That is what they have always done, and that is what they will always do. That is what we will do when we finally find ourselves up there. We will present ourselves to God in worship for eternity.

Returning to the scripture, "The sons of God came and presented themselves before the Lord" is just another way of saying "The angels went to the Throne of God to worship".

So, what made this day different? It was that Satan had joined them. This is the first mention of him returning to the Throne Room since his insurrection that cost heaven one third of its population. Satan had reappeared in that very place. That must have been intense! And what does Satan do best? He deceives.

Satan masquerades as an angel of light, because he used to be one, and he slipped in among the angels acting like one of them. He had experience with "worship" back when he used to be the worship leader in heaven. He knew exactly how to act in the throne room. He, apparently, was hoping to get an audience with God without being noticed by those who had a right to be there.

Let me stop there for a second. You may be asking, "So, why didn't the author of this book just say, 'While the angels were worshiping around the Throne of God, Satan slipped in, masquerading as an angel of light.'?" As stated before, this was before the Prophets, before Moses and maybe around the time of Abraham.

The people in Job's and Abraham's time didn't have an understanding of things like Moses did. Just like Moses didn't have an understanding of things like King David. Just like King David didn't have an understanding of things like the Apostle Paul. Just like Paul didn't have an understanding of things like John on the Isle of Patmos.

When you have a book like this, it is best not to try to draw your own conclusions from it, but to find other clearer passages in the Word and let them define the not so clear passage. That is what is called Good Hermeneutics.

Hermeneutics is the theory and methodology of interpretation, especially of scriptural text. In other words, you let the Word of God interpret the Word of God. That is the best way to find meaning for unclear passages. With every "fuzzy" passage, there are ten other clearer ones that can bring clarity to it.

Uncovering A Matter

Back to what I was saying earlier about "the day", what made this day different was that Satan slipped in and tried to blend in. Satan slips in among them around God's Throne, but, immediately, God points him out. God uncovers the matter, which is typical of Him. How He uncovers it is also typical. He asks a question, "From where do you come?" (Insert shocking thematic music here.)

It is just like when Adam hid himself in the Garden and God asks him, "Where are you?" God knew where Adam was. That wasn't the point. He was uncovering the hidden matter. Jesus also did the same thing. In Matthew 9:33-35 we see Jesus asking his disciples a question He already knew the answer to:

"Then He came to Capernaum. And when He was in the house He asked them, "What was it you disputed among yourselves on the road?" But they kept silent, for on the road they had disputed among themselves who would be the greatest. And He sat down, called the twelve, and said to them, "If anyone desires to be first, he shall be last of all and servant of all."

Jesus knew exactly what they were talking about. Their choice to remain silent only revealed the folly in their silly dispute which is precisely why Jesus asked them the question. When God asks you a question, it is usually because you are being secretive and you need to acknowledge what you are doing.

Here we see that God wasn't about to let Satan get away with anything. He asked him, "From where do YOU come from?" meaning, "No more deception. You're not from here, so reveal who you are and where you are from to all of the angels here!"

Then Satan answered the Lord and said,

"From roaming about on the earth and walking around on it."

Well, he did give an accurate, if vague, answer. The father of all lies, The Deceiver, isn't going to be open and transparent. He always has some agenda that he wants to keep hidden, which you will find out later. He was very vague with his answer, which is why God went straight to the point and asked a more specific question, "Have you considered my servant Job?"

Again, God is uncovering a hidden matter by asking another question. He is not making a suggestion to Satan, which I have heard taught before. I even believed it at one time. No, He is bringing to light Satan's evil plan. He is also not making a wager with the devil.

How foolish is it that this is the popular and accepted view of this dialogue between God and the devil. Since when does God take a gamble on the welfare of His servants? Even worse, since when does God give Satan ideas on how to afflict His saints? That's like giving the kidnapper of your children ideas on how to torture them. That's a bit graphic, but we need to see it for what it is. Step back for a moment from what you've been taught and let's dissect this argument just a bit.

God and Gambling

The first thing wrong with this conclusion is that taking a gamble puts God in subjection to the devil. If God made a bet with Satan, Satan would then hold an even share in determining the outcome, as between equals. God is sovereign – why would He want to lower Himself to someone else's level? We know that will never happen. Second, it goes against the very nature of God. If God was a gambler then we would see multiple accounts of this elsewhere in the Bible and we don't.

I want to take a minute here and establish a black and white truth that has been lost by much of the church. If God calls Himself GOOD, then we must use His definition of GOOD found in the Word to define God's goodness and not some other definition that we have crafted to fit our doctrine.

There is not another GOOD. Good is good and we need to keep it good. God and His Word are one. God does not call something GOOD and then have a separate definition of GOOD that applies to Him. That is called a double standard. That is also called hypocrisy, duplicity and deception. God's truth would then just be smoke and mirrors. His Word would not be irrefutable and infallible anymore. It would be inconsistent, contradictory and incongruous.

If God lived by double standards, then Christ's life, death, burial and resurrection would all be pointless, and we would still be bound for hell. From a legal standpoint it would be fraudulent on the grounds that God had been unclear and inconsistent with His demands on humanity while ruling the Universe by a double standard. He would be going against His own law. This double standard doctrine that many live by today is precisely the trap that Job had fallen into with his skewed beliefs concerning God.

If the Word of God says that He does not play favorites, then to say that He wills to heal some and not all is incorrect. If the Word of God says that physically abusing your children is bad and not good, then saying that God puts sickness on His children to teach them a lesson is a doctrine of devils.

God does not afflict us to teach us or to bring glory to Himself. We don't find it anywhere in the Word of God.

Nevertheless

But you ask, "Doesn't the Word say in John 9:3,

"Jesus answered, 'Neither hath this man sinned, nor his parents: but that the works of God should be made manifest in him.'?"

Not in the original Greek. If you go back to the original Greek, it says something slightly different. The words "but that" were placed there by the Anglican Monks who were the writers of the King James translation of the Greek text. They decided on "but that" which they translated from the Greek word "alla". Alla has been translated in many other passages as "nevertheless". If we put nevertheless in there, it changes the whole meaning. This is how the original Greek meant it which flows much better and gives a clearer understanding of the whole story. Here is the way it should read in Modern English:

John 9:3 revised, *"Jesus answered, 'Neither has this man sinned, nor his parents: nevertheless, the works of God should be made manifest in him. We must do the works of Him who sent Me while it is day. Night is coming when no one can work. As long as I am in the world, I am the light of the world."*

Before I go into the meaning of this passage (actually, I think it just explained itself), I need to add another scripture to the mix.

28

1ˢᵗ Corinthians 4:20 (HCSB), *"For the kingdom of God is not in talk but in power."*

The disciples got caught up in a religious trap. It is the same religious trap that for 2000 years has rendered many in the church ineffectual. The disciples should have been looking for an opportunity to manifest the Kingdom of God, but they got caught up in religious bantering. Here is a blind man. It is the perfect opportunity to display the works of God and bring someone into the kingdom, but they got all religious and judgmental about something that didn't matter.

The discussion on who sinned, him or his parents, was a discussion about generational curses and the sin of the father being visited upon the third and fourth generation. Who knows? Maybe the blind man was the one who started the debate about generational curses, and the disciples got suckered into it. We don't know. What we do know is that they fell for one of the oldest tricks in the devil's playbook.

While they are standing there judging the man, he remained blind to the world and blind to the grace of God. How cruel is that to be standing in front of the blind man talking about him and over him like he is not even there and disputing why he may be blind!

Besides that, they were about to miss their opportunity, until Jesus refocused them on what really mattered. He said, "Never mind who sinned. This is an opportunity for the Works of God to be made manifest in him." That is why Jesus said right after that,

> *"We must do the works of Him who sent Me while it is day. Night is coming when no one can work. As long as I am in the world, I am the light of the world."*

Jesus was saying, "Now is the time to do what I've commissioned you to do which is heal the sick. Your bantering about generational curses and why people are sick or diseased is not the work of God. It is actually hindering the work of God. The work of God is healing the sick and diseased, not judging them, and we must do it while we can."

Seriously?

While I was a student at Christ For The Nations Institute, back in 2000, I ran into a similar situation as the one above. I was with a group of students at a restaurant one evening. There were about eight of us at the table. We were talking about our lectures and classes and had apparently gotten a little loud.

The gentleman at the table next to us said, "Excuse me, I couldn't help overhearing what you all were talking about. . . ", and then he began pouring out his heart to us.

He was hungry for God and was reaching out. He had some unanswered theological questions that he posed to us. Some of them were very valid, while others were a bit frivolous. You know what I am talking about. They went along the same lines as, "Did Adam and Eve have belly buttons?"

Well, it went from answering questions to a full out debate. There were raised voices, frustration and a total lack of focus as to what was supposed to be going on. I knew this man was hungry for God but got sidetracked into foolish bantering which wasn't his fault. They should have recognized this at the table and refocused the man back to his need for Jesus, but continued to foam at the mouth and run off on tangents.

I finally had enough. I said, "Seriously, guys, this man needs an encounter with God and you are talking about 'Easter's not a real Christian Holiday.' Seriously?"

I then told them to chill, and I addressed the man only. After a few minutes of sharing the story of redemption and salvation, this man gave his heart to Jesus. He became born again at his table in the restaurant. It was awesome! Yet an opportunity was almost lost because we neglected to see that this was a set up for the glory of God to be made manifest in this man. We got sidetracked into foolish bantering. Thank God that the moment was saved. Like Jesus said:

"We must do the works of Him who sent Me
while it is day. Night is coming when no one can

work. As long as I am in the world, I am the light of the world."

I went slightly off topic for a minute, but I needed to destroy a lie of the enemy. Here's a little warning: I actually do that quite frequently in the book. A good thing to do is to pray before you pick up this book again. Ask God to help you keep an open mind to truth and things that may have been taught wrongly to you. Ask the Holy Spirit to illuminate it to you.

We need to have a foundation of Who God is and what He does set in place before we begin building any doctrine upon it and interpreting scripture aloof. Without a clear understanding of the character, nature and ways of God, the interpretation of Scripture will often end up in error.

It is perfectly healthy to change your doctrine little by little over time as you come to know the nature and ways of God. The people you have to look out for are the ones that have believed the exact same thing for 30, 40 and 50 years. That shows no sign of growth in their faith and knowledge of God. I will go more in depth about this in *Chapter 9: Let's Talk About Idolatry*, for that Rigidity is actually a sign of Idolatry.

If a teaching says that God does something that is apart from His character, then it is our duty to seek out the truth. Now, let us get back to the story of where God and Satan are discussing Job.

God is not making a wager with the devil, nor is He giving Satan new ideas. Heaven forbid! He is bringing to light Satan's evil plan with a tactic that He always uses to uncover and expose secrets and deceptive ways. God asks a question. And when God asks you a question, it always blows your cover. When God asks you something, it is already too late to hide. God exposed Satan's identity and his reason for slipping into the Throne Room with two questions.

Let me rephrase what God said to Satan in a way that is not so two dimensional, Right in the middle of the deafening sound of a multitude of angels dancing, shouting, worshipping and singing praises before the Throne of God, with the beasts and twenty-four elders, and the thunders and lightening, and the overwhelming glory of God, everything stops and goes completely silent in an instant when God points out the imposter and bellows with His thunderous voice, "You, Satan, are not supposed to be here! You are an imposter! I You didn't come here to give Me worship but to get something from Me! You are here because you are looking at My servant Job! There is none like him on the earth, a blameless and upright man, fearing God and turning away from evil, and yet you are looking at him. Tell all of us here why you are considering him!"

Satan, not missing a beat, answers with a question, ***"Does Job fear God for nothing?"***

I want to stop right there. God says, "Job fears God." And then Satan says, "Does Job fear God for nothing?" First of all, what does "fear" mean here?

I am about to open up a can of worms and destroy some more bad doctrine. You already think you know what can of worms I am referring to, but I can assuredly tell you that you don't. Brace yourself, child of God!

The Faces Of Fear

God said to Satan, "Job fears God." Yet, Satan said to God, "Does Job fear God for nothing?"

Let's go to the Hebrew word that has been translated as "fear" where God says, "Job fears God." The Hebrew word is "yare" (H3373 in Strong's Concordance[4]) which means fearing, reverent and afraid. I'm sure you've heard that before. We are to worship God with a reverential fear.

Now, let's go to the Hebrew word that has been translated as "fear" where Satan asks, "Does Job fear God for nothing?" The Hebrew word is also "yare" but the number is different, H3372, and it adds the words dreadful and terrified to the list. It is the same word, but it is applied differently. I will use some scriptures to bring clarity.

Here are some "yares" that are used for reverence that have the number H3373:

> **Genesis 22:12 (HCSB)** *"Then He said, 'Do not lay a hand on the boy or do anything to him. For now I know that you FEAR (yare H3373) God since you have not withheld your only son from Me.'"*

> **Exodus 18:21(HCSB)** *"But you should select from all the people able men, God-FEARING (yare H3373), trustworthy, and hating bribes."*

The application here is that of reverence and worship. Now here are a few "yares" that are used for terror and dread that have the number H3372:

> **Genesis 3:10 (HCSB)** *"And he said, 'I heard You in the garden, and I was AFRAID (yare H3372) because I was naked, so I hid.'"*

---

[4] Strong's Exhaustive Concordance of the Bible

Genesis 21:17 (HCSB) *"God heard the voice of the boy, and the angel of God called to Hagar from heaven and said to her, 'What's wrong, Hagar? Don't be AFRAID (yare H3372) for God has heard the voice of the boy from the place where he is.'"*

Genesis 15:1 (HCSB) *"After these events, the word of the Lord came to Abram in a vision: 'Do not be AFRAID (yare H3372), Abram. I am your shield; your reward will be very great.'"*

See, the application is quite different. The fear that God references about Job is the healthy reverential or worshipful fear. The fear that Satan references is the fear that God tells you, *"Fear Not in this way!"* In fact, most every verse where God speaks to someone saying, "Fear not!" the H3372 "yare" of terror and dread is used. (A great book to read about the God kind of fear is "The Fear Of The Lord" by John Bevere.)

Also, in these three passages, you see the "fear of loss" at work. I will get into that later. So, we see that Job was terrified of something.

Let's reword what was said a little differently so that we can see what is going on in the discourse between God and Satan:

"Satan, you've considered My servant, Job. Haven't you? There is no one like him on the earth, a blameless and upright man, who worships God and turns away from evil."

Then Satan answered the Lord, *"Is Job terrified of God for nothing?"*

Now we are getting somewhere! With it put this way, Satan isn't addressing what God said. Satan isn't interested in Job's accolades. He's interested in Job's skeletons in the closet. That's what he is after. That's what he is always after. He doesn't care about our good points. He's after our frailties.

Like A Roaring Lion

Let's back up a little for a minute. Satan told God he was out prowling the earth, which is backed up in scripture in 1st Peter 5:8 (NLT[5]),

> *"Be careful! Watch out for attacks from the Devil, your great enemy. He prowls around like a roaring lion, looking for some victim to devour."*

In nature, lions look for the weak, the lame, the young and the foolish. They seek out prey that already has a weakness, and then they exploit that weakness and bring them down. Satan is compared to a lion for the same reason. He goes around, studying us, his enemy, looking for our weak spot. And we all have one, some tiny chink in the armor of our salvation, some "little thing" that allows him to get a foothold in our lives.

It's human nature – the nature we, as Christians, are always trying to conquer as we put on the Mind of Christ and become more like Jesus than ourselves. And in Job, Satan found his opportunity – fear. Let's now address what Satan said to God.

So, what does this mean, "Is Job terrified of God for nothing?" To understand what this means, we must first understand the plan of the enemy. What is the plan of the enemy? To steal, kill and destroy (John 10:10). He will use every means possible to do that. He will even go to God and argue scripture and law to get a legal standing to steal, kill and destroy, which is precisely what he was doing here.

Faith vs. Fear

One thing we must understand is that fear is the Devil's territory. When you operate in fear, the Devil has legal right to put his hand on you. Faith causes God to move on our behalf, while fear causes Satan

---

[5] New Living Translation

to move against our behalf. I like the way Andy Andrews puts it in "The Traveler's Gift":

> *"All men are driven by faith or fear – one or the other – for both are the same. Faith or fear is the expectation of an event that hasn't come to pass or the belief in something that cannot be seen or touched. A man of fear lives always on the edge of insanity. A man of faith lives in perpetual reward."*
>
> **(Andy Andrews, The Traveler's Gift – page 149)**

So, restating what Andy Andrews said, Faith and Fear are both the expectation of something that hasn't come to pass. While both of them are the same in that aspect, they both are different in two ways. One way is that fear brings to pass what isn't real, while faith brings to pass what God has already provided for us in His Word. The second way that they are different is that faith and fear activate a different set of characters. Again, faith activates and accesses what God has provided for us and causes God to move on our behalf, while fear causes Satan to move against our behalf.

Getting back to what Satan said, in order to understand what he intended by "for nothing" we need to read what he said next.

> *"Have you not made a hedge about him and his house and all that he has, on every side? You have blessed the work of his hands, and his possessions have increased in the land. But put forth your hand now and touch all that he has; he will surely curse You to Your face."*

Satan is saying, *"The opportunity and right I should have to destroy him because of his terror and fear is wasted because You protect him. Because he lives in fear, he is in my territory and should be under my jurisdiction. I have legal right to touch him because of his fear. Now stop protecting him and let me touch him! And when You do I will watch him curse You to Your face!"*

In the next chapter we will look at what transpires when God gives Satan exactly what he wanted.

Now There Was A Day

"Now there was a day when his sons and daughters [were] eating and drinking wine in their oldest brother's house; and a messenger came to Job and said, 'The oxen were plowing and the donkeys feeding beside them, when the Sabeans raided [them] and took them away--indeed they have killed the servants with the edge of the sword; and I alone have escaped to tell you!"

While he [was] still speaking, another also came and said, "The fire of God fell from heaven and burned up the sheep and the servants, and consumed them; and I alone have escaped to tell you!"

While he [was] still speaking, another also came and said, "The Chaldeans formed three bands, raided the camels and took them away, yes, and killed the servants with the edge of the sword; and I alone have escaped to tell you!"

While he [was] still speaking, another also came and said, "Your sons and daughters [were] eating and drinking wine in their oldest brother's house, "and suddenly a great wind came from across the wilderness and struck the four corners of the house, and it fell on the young people, and they are dead; and I alone have escaped to tell you!"
(Job 1:13-19 NKJV)

Let me point out that it is said once again, "Now there was a day when. . ." This is really significant here. The reason why it is so significant is that there is a common belief and teaching that right after Satan acquired the Lord's permission that he immediately brought destruction upon Job. There is a big problem with that teaching. Let's rewind a second.

When is the first "Now there was a day" mentioned? It is mentioned concerning the day that Satan went to God for permission to harm Job. The second time that "Now there was a day" was mentioned is when Satan did rain destruction upon Job. What does that mean? It means that there was a substantial amount of time between when Satan got permission and the time he actually did the dirty deed. Why is that significant? Because Satan needed to know exactly what he was allowed to do before he came up with a plan. What is the point in formulating a plan of action before you know what your boundaries are? It's called counting your eggs before they hatch. Satan is no rookie. His first great war strategy involved taking a third of the population of heaven. I'm sure that involved quite a bit of planning as well. He is not to be underestimated.

And notice in the case with Job that Satan didn't just rush in. No. Satan, just like any great war strategist, counted all the costs, looked at what resources he had at his disposal, ran all possible formulas, consulted with his top generals, did test runs, worked out all the kinks and had dress rehearsals right up until the day he was to carry out his master plan. The timing in this whole ordeal is absolutely astounding. Don't believe me? Let's take a look at every little detail in this masterpiece disaster.

I think that it is necessary to quote once more the verse concerning Job's assets.

> *(Job 1:3) "His estate included 7,000 sheep, 3,000 camels, 500 yoke of oxen, 500 female donkeys, and a very large number of servants. Job was the greatest man among all the people of the east."*

Wrap those numbers around your head. It's not 7 sheep, 3 camels, 5 yoke of oxen and 5 female donkeys. Look at all the zeros. The total number of animals are 11,500. I grew up in the south around farms and cattle ranches. In order to have that many animals, in a time period without hay bales and tractors, you would need hundreds if not thousands of acres of land to feed them. Not only that but, because of the lack of technology, you would need a very large number of hired hands to take care of them.

Considering the hostile people groups that surrounded Job's Estate (I will get to that in a minute.) these hired hands would not only be skilled in taking care of these large numbers of animals, but they would also be highly skilled in the art of combat. Job was the wealthiest man in the region. I'm sure he hired the best of the best. This brings me to another issue that many don't consider.

The Body of Satan

I could write a whole other book on this subject. Actually, I plan on it. This truth is so simple and yet so overlooked; not just in the Book of Job. I'm going to take a big rabbit trail that you will appreciate.

About 5 years ago God had me study the book of Revelations, Daniel, Ezekiel and other prophets who dealt with the end times. One of the things I came to realize about Satan is that he is powerless in the Earth without a physical body. In order for you to understand what I am talking about, I need to talk about Jesus.

When Jesus ascended to Heaven, He promised us that He would send us the Holy Spirit. The Holy Spirit would endue us with power. Power to do what? To do what Christ did in the Earth: heal the sick, raise the dead, cast out demons, etc. In other words, we would be Jesus to the world.

I like what Miles Monroe said when he spoke to us at Bible School. He said, and I am paraphrasing, *"Notice that we are not called The Body of Jesus. No. We are called the Body of Christ. Jesus is in Heaven, while the Holy Spirit is in the Earth working through His Body; the Body of Christ."*

Is the Body of Christ one person? No. The Body of Christ is made up of millions and millions of people starting from the Day of

Pentecost 2000 years ago coming to the present day Church and on until the Second Coming of Christ when He begins His Thousand Year Reign.

Satan, since the birth of kingdoms in the Earth, has had a body that he has used to carry out his plans. This body has been comprised of many kingdoms that have risen and fallen from power. What does he use his body to do? One of its main goals is to oppress the people of God, whether it be Israel, the Church or, in this case, Job. The body of Satan has had a few names. In Daniel and in Revelation it is given the name "The Beast". Popular eschatology tells you that the Beast is one person, but Gabriel told Daniel that a beast, when it comes to prophetic dreams and visions, is a kingdom. Just to make a point here, Gabriel told Daniel what it was, and we never see it reclassified anywhere else in scripture or questioned by any other prophet, not even John on the Isle of Patmos. Why? Because they had the Book of Daniel as a reference guide to what a Beast in prophecy represented. There I go again challenging the status quo.

There have been many people groups, nations, empires and kingdoms that have been a part of this body of Satan: Egypt, Assyria, Babylon, Mede, Persia, Greece, Rome and Islamic Imperialism just to name a few. All of these kingdoms have oppressed the saints of God in one way or another. AND all of these kingdoms were up to their eyeballs in idol worship. Now that I've laid some groundwork for my next point, let's get back to kingdoms that Satan used to bring destruction and devastation on the Job household.

Job's Hostile Neighbors

Who are the people groups whom Satan used to pull off his grand scheme? The first ones mentioned are the Sabeans. Who are the Sabeans? Wikipedia – Sabaeans says:

> *"The Sabaeans or Sabeans were an ancient people speaking an Old South Arabian language who lived in what is today Yemen, in the south west of the Arabian Peninsula.*

40

Some scholars suggest a link between the Sabaeans and the Biblical land of Sheba, and would dismiss any link or confusion with the Sabians. . . ."

Phew! Glad they cleared that up! *rolls eyes* Continuing. . .

"The Sabaean people were South Arabian people. . . . involved in the extremely lucrative spice trade, especially frankincense and myrrh.

They left behind many inscriptions in the monumental Musnad (Old South Arabian) alphabet, as well as numerous documents in the cursive Zabūr script." **(Wikipedia – Sabaeans)**

They were South Arabian spice traders. What was their government like?

"Their territory was situated between those of the Mineans and Cattabanes; and their capital, Mariaba, stood on the summit of a wooded hill. The country, like those adjoining, was a flourishing monarchy, with beautiful temples and palaces, and with houses which resembled those of the Egyptians. The mode of succession to the throne was peculiar in that the heir apparent was not the son of the king, but the first son born to a noble after the monarch's accession. The king himself was also the judge; but he was not allowed to leave the palace under penalty of being stoned to death by the people." **(JewishEncyclopedia.com – Sabeans, In The Classical Writers)**

I can safely say that no one was pining away to be the king in this culture. Imprisoned in the royal palace under penalty of death if they escaped? Wow. That is messed up. That might be why they didn't last very long as a culture. Seriously.

I can hear the exchange between the nobles and the new monarch.

Noble: Guess what? Congratulations! You are the new King!

New King: No! I like my life! I have a successful spice trading business! Life is good! I never wanted to be king!

Noble: You know the rules. You were the first one born after the last king came to power.

New King: What happened to the last king anyway? He was only king for four months.

Noble: Suicide.

New King: That's what happened to the last three kings. Do you think that maybe we are doing this wrong? What makes you think that I won't do it?

Noble: We have removed all sharp objects from the palace. There is no way you can harm yourself.

New King: . . . *sigh*

Lastly, what about their religion? This is actually a very important question, seeing that Satan put this whole fiasco together. I am not going to bore you with the long list of gods and goddesses that this culture worshipped. They, just like many other cultures, borrowed from other cultures and the nations that surrounded them. (They should have also borrowed how kingly succession was supposed to happen as well.) There were 16 gods and 4 goddesses that they commonly worshipped. They were gods of war, fortune, wine, sun, moon, stars nature, hearing, gazelles (yes, I said gazelles), generic, sex, etc. If I listed them for you, your eyes would glaze over. You can reference "JewishEncyclopedia.com – Sabeans, Deitites" if you are still interested.

Seriously though, one or two idols are hard enough to keep up with. How do you appease so many gods and goddesses? Talk about being conflicted! That had to be exhausting. Of course, Satan is going to use the most wicked and depraved people of the region to carry out his diabolical plan. The Sabeans were steeped in idol worship and wickedness. It wouldn't take much for Satan to garner the resources of this people group. One more quote will bring this all together:

> *"The military texts, in their accounts of successful raids on and repulses of other marauding tribes."* **(JewishEncyclopedia – Sabeans, Commerce Agriculture and Religion)**

They were skilled and trained in the art of raiding other tribes and peoples. We see now why Satan chose this group of people to do his dirty work. It said the Sabeans raided the oxen and donkeys and took them away. There were 500 yoke of oxen which is 1000 oxen because one yoke holds two oxen, and 500 female donkeys. That's 1500 large grazing animals. How many men were needed to pull that stunt off? Sure, if you own a farm with that many animals, you might be able to move them with minimal manpower, but this was a raiding party who had to quickly get away with steeling 1,500 large animals; 1000 of them in yokes. That was no small matter.

Have you ever tried to move a donkey that wasn't yours? I've owned a female donkey before. They will move when they want to. If they don't know you, you are out of luck. So, if you have 500 stubborn female donkeys, that is going to take at least 200 or more men to do it, not to mention the 1000 oxen. I would estimate it took at least 500 skilled men to pull this off with moving the oxen and donkeys. That's just to move the animals.

You may be saying, *"Well, couldn't they have put the donkeys on carts to move them?"* Putting them on a cart to move them is so much harder than just moving them. Their stubbornness is amplified exponentially when you add a confined space to it.

Like I said, not only did they take the animals, but they also killed all the servants that were responsible for the care and protection of these animals. Well, all of them except for one fleeing coward, of course. Again, most likely, Job hired the best of the best that were skilled in the art of combat. They knew how to use a sword, just like most people in that day and age.

This adds to the size of the raiding party. They had to slaughter the huge number of servants, and then when they were done with that they had to quickly remove the animals. Are you getting the picture here?

Let's look at the next people group Satan used, which were the Chaldeans. Maybe they weren't as kooky as the Sabeans were. One can only hope.

"Chaldea or Chaldaea. . . was a marshy land located in south eastern Mesopotamia which came to rule Babylon briefly. Tribes of Semitic settlers who arrived in the region from the 10th Century BC became known as the Chaldeans or the Chaldees. . . Though the name came to be commonly used to refer to the whole of southern Mesopotamia, Chaldea proper was in fact the vast plain in the far south east formed by the deposits of the Euphrates and the Tigris, extending to about four hundred miles along the course of these rivers, and about a hundred miles in average width. . .

Chaldea as the name of a country is used in two different senses. In the early period it was the name of a small territory in southern Babylonia extending along the northern and probably also the western shores of the Persian Gulf." **(Wikipedia – Chaldea)**

We get a picture of where they were located. What about their religious activity?

"Chaldean mythology is the collective name given to Sumerian, Assyrian and Babylonian mythologies, although Chaldea did not comprehend the whole territory inhabited by those peoples. Also called Chaldaic mythology.

The Sumerians practised a polytheistic religion, with anthropomorphic gods or goddesses representing forces or presences in the world, much as in the later Greek mythology. The gods originally created humans as servants for themselves, but freed them when they became too much to handle."

(economicexpert.com – Chaldean mythology)

So, we see that the Chaldeans had an influence on Greek Mythology. They weren't as kooky, but idol worship is still idol worship. According to Infoplease.com there were 7 gods and goddesses that you will recognize:

> "...the gods of the seven planets called in the Latin language Saturn, Jupiter, Mars, Apollo [i.e. the Sun], Mercury, Venus, and Diana [i.e. the Moon]."

What? No gazelle worship? How unoriginal.

Both the Sabeans and the Chaldeans were heavy into idol worship. This is a contrast to Job and his worship of Jehovah.

Let's read the passage in Job once more about the Chaldean raid:

> "The Chaldeans formed three bands, raided the camels and took them away, yes, and killed the servants with the edge of the sword..."

The Chaldeans formed three bands. A band, in this case, is a troop or a cavalry unit corresponding to an infantry company. They formed three military units and raided Job's land. They killed all of the servants but one, another fleeing coward, and then absconded with the camels which numbered 3,000. That is a lot of camels.

We have two separate and culturally different nations of wicked, idol worshippers who sent their militaries in to devastate the Job household. Are you getting the picture yet? The Sebeans depleted Job's oxen and donkeys to zero, killing everyone, on one side, and the Chaldeans depleted Job's camels to zero, killing everyone, on the other side on the same day within the same hour. That's not all. We haven't got to the sheep yet.

Fire fell from heaven and burned up 7,000 sheep and the servants who had charge overt them. FIRE FELL FROM HEAVEN. That is a lot of flaming sheep! My brain instantly went all cartoonish to thousands of running sheep on fire. That's my ridiculous brain for you. Seriously though, that's quite a massacre. It wasn't just the sheep, but also the servants who burned to death. Well, one fireproof coward escaped.

Satan is pretty slick. We have learned that Satan does everything he can to make people think that the destruction brought by him was actually God's fault. This is one of his favorite things to do. This time he mimics God. Don't we see God doing this elsewhere in the Old Testament? There's the story of where Elijah set up an altar to Jehovah and the prophets of Ba'al also set up an altar.

> *"Then the fire of the LORD fell, and consumed*
> *the burnt sacrifice, and the wood, and the stones,*
> *and the dust, and licked up the water that [was] in*
> *the trench."* **(1 Kings 18:38 KJV)**

Satan accomplished two major things here with raining fire from heaven. The first thing is he set God up, so to speak, in making this look like an act of God. He forged God's signature on the deal. That way no one would be able to say it was not God who did this. No wonder everyone unquestionably blamed God for this! This is a signature move of Satan and the televangelists fall for it every time. He will wreak havoc and then somehow put a God spin on it.

How many times have we fallen for it without even seeking God on it? Hurricane Katrina? The Earthquake in Haiti? The earthquake and tsunami in Japan? You know what I am talking about. The televangelist puppets are the ones who spout out this junk and the church drinks their punch. I go a lot more in depth with this in the chapter on Cultural Hindrances.

In making it look as if this all was an act of God, Satan isolated Job. How did he do this? When the people believed that it was an act of God they decided not to help Job. Job was, in their eyes, being punished by God. Why go against the judgment of God to help the one being judged?

The second thing that was accomplished by Satan was even more profound. What did Job use the sheep for? They were what he used to worship Jehovah. He used them to make sacrifice in the early morning and all throughout the day. He had 7,000 of them! Satan took out his worship! This is also a signature move of Satan. If Satan can take out your worship, you are pretty much done for.

Let's combine the two things Satan accomplished. He made it look as if God was not pleased with Job's worship, so much so that

46

He rained His judgment down upon him. That kind of gives me a sick feeling in my stomach.

The last thing Satan did, which was his icing on the cake, was to destroy Job's family while they were having one of their drunken parties that Job was fearful would get them creamed by God. Are you feeling the weight of this yet? Here is something that I learned about Satan when I was a teenager that is pretty heavy.

We learn in the New Testament that Satan is also known as the prince of the power of the air.

> *"Wherein in time past ye walked according to the course of this world, according to the prince of the power of the air, the spirit that now worketh in the children of disobedience:"* **(Ephesians 2:2 KJV)**

That sounds like a high and lofty title, but let's break it down. What is the power of the air, or should I say the power BEHIND the air? THE WIND. And the wind controls the weather. Satan is the Prince or Ruler of the Wind. He can control the wind which maneuvers the weather. This is pretty profound, yet it makes perfect sense.

The Devil's Tornado

I had a dream in the mid 1990's where I was standing in the street in front of my house (I was a teenager at the time) with my mother, father and brother. The weather grew dark and out of nowhere a florescent green tornado appeared in front of me. In the middle of this tornado was a pair of eyes. I knew that Satan was in this tornado. My family ran in the house, but I stopped at the door and turned around to look at the tornado. I rebuked Satan and told him to leave my family alone. The tornado backed up to the end of the street, but never took its eyes off of me. That was the end of the dream.

A few days later there was some bad weather in our area due to a hurricane that was traveling up the coastline but not making landfall. It brought many tornadoes with it. I was standing outside in front of the house with my family when we noticed what appeared to be a funnel cloud forming directly above our house. Everyone panicked and ran in the house but me.

Without fear I pointed at the funnel cloud and said, "I rebuke you in Jesus' Name. You will not touch down here. You will go over there." I had pointed into the woods in front of our house. The funnel cloud, which was not moving, then moved quickly in the direction I pointed. It landed in a trailer park just past the woods and destroyed many houses. Maybe I should have said, "Peace, Be Still." Hey, it was my first time commanding a storm to move. Oops.

I have commanded many storms since then and a majority of the time they have listened. Not all storms are spun by the enemy, but there are some that you can tell by the Spirit of God that they have an assignment on them. When the Spirit quickens us to this, we can command them to cease and they will listen.

Satan's Precision

I said all that to say this: Satan directed a storm with great precision to the house where all of Job's children were. The storm didn't affect the region. It didn't destroy the houses nearby. It destroyed one specific house which had Job's family in it. It carried out its assignment with great accuracy. The storm did, however, spare one servant that could be the bearer of bad news to Job.

Let's do a recap here. Job had a fear that God would destroy his family due to their riotousness. Satan initiated a plan that involved two neighboring nations who sent in their militaries that wiped out all of his servants and herded 4,500 of his animals back home with them. He rained down fire from heaven, imitating Jehovah in front of everyone quite convincingly as you will see later, and destroyed Job's flock of 7,000 sheep which were what Job used to worship Jehovah.

He sent a demonic whirlwind to one house alone that was facilitating a drunken party hosted by Job's ten children and killed them all. This happened in view of everyone in the region. Everyone saw it. You can be sure that Satan put on a good show. News of this traveled far and wide throughout the region that Job, Jehovah's man of the hour, was just utterly betrayed by the very God he worshipped because of the wickedness of his children.

Satan had it so meticulously planned out, that fire fell from heaven consuming 7,000 sheep, while at the same exact moment two culturally different neighboring nations raided Job's land, killing the servants and taking 3,000 camels, 500 yoke of oxen and 500 donkeys, while at the same exact moment a whirlwind destroyed Job's houses and killed his children, and then each servant that survived arrives just as the servant before was finished telling Job the evil report. See what a master mind he is?

Satan spared the life of one servant in each place so that they could be the bearer of bad news. Satan always seems to spare the bearers of bad news. Have you ever noticed that? Here is an example: You just got diagnosed with something. Let's say it's colon cancer. News travels of this and the roaches start coming out of the woodwork. You know what I mean. You run into them at the supermarket and they say something like, *"I heard you had colon cancer. That's terrible. All of my uncles, aunts, nieces, nephews, brothers and sisters died slow, agonizing and painful deaths from colon cancer. Right before they died, each one of them was begging God to kill them. It's like the people in the Alien movies who were impregnated by the aliens, where they would say "Kill me! Kill me! Kill me!" right before the aliens burst out of their chests and they all died. It's a terrible thing. Bless your heart."*

And yet they alone did not get the cancer. Why? Satan spared the bearer of bad news. Yes, this is a great exaggeration, but I wanted you to get the point. Watch what news you herald.

My mother, before she passed away from pancreatic cancer, went through the same thing. Someone sent her a card that said, *"God chose you for this suffering."* WHAT?! And then numerous people came to her and said, *"Now you know it is going to get terrible right at the end, right? You will welcome death."*

Seriously? That is not at all what you should be saying to someone who has a few months left to live. Good grief. Back to the story.

There is one among many things that Satan is good at, and it is called Strategic Warfare. What is Satan's plan for humanity again? It is to steal from us, kill us and destroy all we have. He is the master of destruction.

Let's make something clear here. I've heard it said over and over again by preachers in the pulpit that Satan is stupid. That is the farthest thing from the truth. Satan is the second smartest individual on planet Earth. He is more than six thousand years old. He has had all that time to develop and master his strategies and plans. He has had an amazing success rate in this world. If you still aren't sure of this, look at history. Satan likes the fact that you think that he is stupid. Notice that he hasn't challenged you on it. Why is that? So that you will underestimate him and not pay attention. The Word of God says *"Do not be ignorant of the enemy's devices and schemes."* He is Mad Scientist Brilliant.

Satan has a plan for your life. He has it mapped and planned out. He has short and long term goals he wants to achieve in bringing your destruction. He doesn't sleep or take breaks. He is at this very moment watching everything that you do. He is observing how you react to his latest influence or circumstance and putting it in his daily

_____ (insert your name) Journal. He is constantly modifying and perfecting his plans against you. He will never back off, relent or slow in his plan to destroy you. Ever.

With that in mind, it is your responsibility to pray, to seek the Lord, to worship God, to read the Word and to get into God's presence. You are responsible for proactively making choices of where you will go, what you will do and what you will not do. You do not have the right to get upset at God when you just let things happen. If you don't live on purpose, then your life will be a series of accidents, calamities and bad choices. You will constantly be taken by surprise by the wrong things and be left devastated. I myself can attest to that.

So many believers live just this way. Sure, they love Jesus and go to church on Sunday, but that's about it. They don't study the Word on a regular basis. They don't worship. They don't pray. They don't seek direction from the Lord. Then, when it all falls apart for the umpteenth time, they blame God. This sounds like I used to be. I think I've said enough on this for now. Let's get back to the story.

So, Job went from being God's man of the hour, the wealthiest man on the planet who had everything any man could ever want, to a man supposedly rejected by God, destitute, childless and homeless in an instant. Even in our day with all of the technology, computers, internet and fast access, a stunt like that would take a very long time to plan. The execution of it would be a one shot deal and the man power and budget needed for this is staggering to think about.

I thank God that Satan isn't allowed to just execute whatever plan that he wants to. There are certain boundaries that he isn't allowed to cross. God's Word restricts him, which brings us to the next part of the story.

Legality And Loopholes

So God lifted His protection and Satan came in like a flood and destroyed everything. God did not have a legal leg to stand on to help Job because Job operated in fear, which ties God's hands, so to speak.

What do I mean by a legal leg to stand on? Isn't God the Almighty? How could God step aside for Satan like this? The answer is, when we operate outside of His Word, we operate outside of His protection. We become vulnerable, exploitable – and the Devil is right there waiting for us when we move out of that protection.

The issue we see here is that Job was the first and last person ever mentioned in the Word that remained protected while operating outside of God's Word. God was having mercy on Job until Satan threw God's Word, so to speak, in God's face. And, God being a God of His Word, had to comply.

Also, there is no record of Job having a covenant with God. He did not have a promise from God like Abraham did. Job knew God (possibly learning of him from Abraham or one of Noah's descendants) and worshipped him, but it was something he initiated, unlike God's relationship with Abraham where God was the one who sought Abram out. There is no record of the Devil ever bringing harm to Abraham. Why? He couldn't touch him because of the Abrahamic Covenant.

There is no record of Satan approaching God concerning the people of Israel. Why? Because they were protected under the Mosaic Covenant. Today, God offers us a New Covenant of salvation through the blood of Jesus. However, the New Covenant is different from the others because He also has given us the Holy Spirit, which gives us power (Acts 1:8, NIV[6]). In the other covenants, obedience meant

---

[6] New International Version

blessing and disobedience meant cursing (Deuteronomy 11:27-28, KJV[7]). But once Jesus became the sacrifice for our sins, Satan was defeated and his power over believers was broken.

Unfortunately for most believers, knowing he is a defeated foe and believing he has no power over us isn't as easy as you would think. The New Testament is full of encouragement for us in our battle against the "mind games" of the Enemy. In our Christian walk, when does Satan attack us? It's usually when we have lost confidence with God, or when we've stepped outside of faith and into fear. God only responds to our faith. Outside of faith, we are helpless, but inside of faith, we have God's protection.

Here are a few passages that bring the point home.

> **Psalm 27:1 (NLT[8])** *"The LORD is my light and my salvation— so why should I be afraid? The LORD protects me from danger— so why should I tremble?"*

> **1 John 4:18 (NIV),** *"There is no fear in love. But perfect love drives out fear, because fear has to do with punishment. The one who fears is not made perfect in love."*

So if God is love, as 1 John 4:18 tells us, then to be made perfect in love is to become like God. And if love drives out fear, we cannot live in fear if the love of God is overflowing in our hearts. If God's love is overflowing in your heart, there's no room for fear. I will expound more on this in a later chapter.

I want to point out again that God was out of character for protecting Job while Job was living in terror and dread. We don't see that happening anywhere else in the Bible. The occurrence with Job is the first and last time we see it. It was a loop hole so to speak until Satan challenged it. For God to continue to bless Job in his fear would be for God to condone his fear. To keep protecting us in our fear is to keep us from being responsible for our decisions.

---

[7] King James Version
[8] New Living Translation

54

Based on this, I think the question should not be "Why did God lift His protection off of Job?" but rather "Why did God keep His protection on Job for so long before lifting it?"

Growing Up And Facing The World

You can relate what happened to Job with planting a garden. There are right ways and wrong ways to plant a garden. The wrong way is to scatter the seeds on top of the ground and hope for the best. The birds would be there in 5 seconds flat to take the spoils!

One right way to plant a garden is to plant your seeds inside your house in little containers. You baby them until they sprout. You give them more sunlight, but still protect them inside. With each stage of growth you protect them until the time is right to plant them. If you continue to protect them inside and don't plant them, their growth would be stunted and they would never reach their full potential. You wind up harming them by over-protecting them.

Baby trees are the same way. You plant them. You support them with stakes and ropes. You put a close fence around the trunk. You water them and constantly look after them until they are ready to stand on their own. When they become a certain age and strength, you remove the stakes and ropes. You remove the fence and you then let the tree alone to do its own thing.

I think Job can be compared to this analogy. God planted Job and protected him. Job increased in wealth, prosperity and posterity. All the while, Job still remained in fear and never dealt with it. I believe that God continued to protect Job to give him a chance to get it right and step out of fear and into faith. He gave him a very long time to get it right, but there comes a time when the tiny tree becomes a mighty oak and needs to stand on its own. Who knows? Maybe fear didn't become an issue until right before Satan challenged God on it. We don't know. What we do know is that God went out of His way to protect Job for as long as He could.

Satan went to God and said, "You gave him a chance. You protected him, and he still has not dealt with his fear. Now it is my turn. Remove the stakes and ropes and fence from around Your mighty oak."

Job had a lifetime to deal with his fear but did not. There comes a time when we all have to face the music. There comes a time when our parents can no longer protect us from the world. There comes a time when we have to be adults and stand on our own two feet and take responsibility. Are our parents wicked for letting us become adults and experience life? No. That's what parents are supposed to do. It is a natural part of life.

The same thing goes with God. It was time for Job to weather the storm on the foundation he had built. If God continued to protect Job in his fear, sooner or later his fear unchecked and not dealt with would have destroyed him anyway. It would have been self-sabotage. What a sobering truth!

So, what I believe we are seeing here is not a God who lifted his protection from a blameless man to give Satan free course. No! What we see here is a loving, compassionate and patient God who went above and beyond the call of duty by protecting His blameless servant, Job, for the longest time possible. God was giving Job a chance to get things right with his faith.

I am sure that Satan tried many times to destroy Job to no avail because of God's protection. It is by focusing on how long He provided that protection, rather than the fact that He lifted it, where we discover a grand truth!

Scripture may not have been penned at the time, but God and His Word are one. His Word was in the beginning, even if it wasn't on paper. So, Job was operating outside of faith and in fear which means he was outside of the boundaries of God's Word and God was still protecting him. This is the only occurrence of this ever recorded.

This is also the first record of Satan coming into the Throne Room to bring it up to God. When you find a place where something is mentioned for the first time in the Word of God, it is important to take note of it. Satan didn't always accuse and there was a first time when he started to. I believe that this was it. I believe that is why God had to point him out to the other angels. I also believe that is why God, right after this, goes into covenant with Abraham.

Satan came up with a new move to hurt humanity, so God ushered in a new way to protect humanity. He cut a covenant with Abraham.

Maybe that is why Job is not the father of our faith, but Abraham is. Who knows? What we do know is that after Job's unfortunate situation, we don't see this ever happening again. My opinion is that I think God took precautionary measures by going into covenant with Abraham.

The only other passage there is concerning Satan going before God and accusing the saints is found in Revelation12:10:

> *"And I heard a loud voice saying in heaven,*
> *Now is come salvation, and strength, and the*
> *kingdom of our God, and the power of his Christ:*
> *for the accuser of our brethren is cast down, which*
> *accused them before our God day and night."*

Here we see that Satan going to God in accusation of us was a regular occurrence until salvation, strength and the Kingdom of God had manifested through Jesus Christ. We, as saints, can no longer be accused. The gavel was dropped. The verdict was read and the case is closed. We are redeemed. Let's get back to the story.

The Fear of Loss

I mentioned earlier the fear of loss. Job had a fear of loss. Just like every time God says to one of His servants, "Fear not!" there is an element of the fear of loss. Where do we see this fear of loss first mentioned?

> **Job 1:4 (HCSB)** *"His sons used to have*
> *banquets, each at his house in turn. They would*
> *send an invitation to their three sisters to eat and*
> *drink with them. Whenever a round of banqueting*
> *was over, Job would send for his children and*
> *purify them, rising early in the morning to offer*

burnt offerings for all of them. For Job thought: Perhaps my children have sinned, having cursed God in their hearts. This was Job's regular practice."

Now it is not blatantly said here, but we see that Job had a fear that something terrible might happen to his children because they may have sinned and cursed God in their hearts. In their hearts! Not out of their mouths or by their actions, but in their hearts. Job continually sacrificed burnt offerings just in case his children secretly cursed God in their hearts. That says something. We've looked at "before"; now let's look at "after".

Job 3:25 (HCSB) *"For the thing I feared has overtaken me, and what I dreaded has happened to me."*

There is "yare H3772" at work! The thing he dreaded has happened to him!

Job lived in terror that God would take away everything that He gave to Job. He feared that God would strike his children dead if they weren't constantly made right by his burnt offerings. He feared that because of secret thoughts that may not have been Godly, his children would be destroyed by God. He greatly feared it and took precautionary measures every day very early in the morning. He woke up thinking about it every single day! And when it finally did happen, he said, *"For the thing I feared has overtaken me, and what I dreaded has happened to me."*

It was like he was saying, *"I KNEW IT! I KNEW IT! I FEARED THAT GOD WOULD DO THIS, AND, SURE ENOUGH, IT HAPPENED! Maybe if I had sacrificed more, or rose up a little earlier in the morning this would not have happened!"*

He was so terrified by the thought of his children being destroyed by God that he had an excess of 7000 sacrificial sheep which I believe were specifically for the purification of his children. 7000 sheep for one household! For crying out loud!

When it finally happened, Job immediately said, *"The Lord gave and the Lord took away."* He never asked God what happened. He never asked God to fix what happened. He never had a question about it. He was sure that he knew exactly why and how and Who! The thing he dreaded, he thought, had overtaken him! (We are getting closer to addressing this misstatement by Job, but keep reading, we have a bit more to discuss first.)

Strategy and Efficacy

On a side note here, isn't it interesting that Job was afraid that his children might curse God in their hearts, but Satan was more concerned with getting Job to curse God? This brings to light something else on the character and ways of Satan.

Why would Satan be so hell bent on getting Job to crack and curse God when it would have been so much easier to get Job's children to do it? Job was even sacrificing daily to keep his children from doing it. Why did Satan choose a hard target? It is because Job was considered by God to be the most blameless and upright man on the face of the earth. He carried a great influence in his community.

To get Job to curse God would be getting the whole community to follow suit. Job was incredibly wealthy and very influential within his community. I'm sure that the family business was far reaching throughout the region for scripture says that he was the wealthiest man in the region. Because of that he most likely employed many of the people in the area and was a great influence on the town's economy. He carried a lot of weight. Everyone was watching Job, so if Job fell, so would a great majority of those who were watching.

It is a great lesson for those who desire a leadership role in the Body of Christ. When a church member falls, not many are affected. When a pastor, elder, worship leader or missionary falls, it sends shockwaves through the ministry and community they are a part of for years to come.

What is lost when a leader falls usually is not recovered for a very long time. Satan had an invested interest in bringing Job to ruin.

Think of the damage that could have been done if Job had given up on God and cursed him. Satan was going for what would bring the greatest windfall.

The devil is a great strategist after all. While he may always be looking for an easy kill, Satan is also on the loose looking for a kill that will ultimately cause the greatest damage. He is like a skilled hunter who goes after the most elusive and cunning prey. Let's get back to Job holding fast to his integrity.

Unwavering Devotion?

There is still a supposed ray of light shining in this, though. Job did not curse God. God had lifted His protection away and let the enemy come in and completely destroy everything good in Job's life and yet Job did not curse God. In fact Job did something remarkable. Even though Job blamed God for his calamity, he still blessed the Name of the Lord. His reverence of God remained intact. How is that even possible?

Job had such a devotion to God that even in the midst of absolute destruction, which he thought was brought upon by God, he was unshakable in his devotion and worship to God! I'll tell you how it might be possible. It could be the very same thing that got him into this whole mess; terror and dread.

It's the same reason that devout worshipers of the Indian goddess of death, Kali, remain so devoted to the worship of her. She is absolutely terrible and dark and evil and merciless, and yet her devout followers are unwavering in their devotion and worship to her. They live in absolute terror and dread of her! They believe that if they waver in their devotion and worship of her in any way that she will strike them down.

It is the same tactic that is used in some Christian circles. "Hellfire and Brimstone" may bring a great many to the Cross and keep them walking a fine line, but the result is a lifetime of pain, loss, sickness, death, hatred, fear and open season for the enemy to wreak havoc on the saints.

60

If you don't believe me, just go to a "Hellfire and Brimstone" church service on "Testimony" night and listen to the older saints who have lived with this terror as they "testify" about their God. Look around, while you are at it and you will notice the heaviness on the saints. You may even notice manifestations of chronic physical infirmities on a large scale.

A Not-So-Celebratory Celebration

Here's a little story to illustrate what I am talking about. I was having dinner at one of the local pizza restaurants one night where something caught my attention. When I was seated, I noticed to the left of me a church group that was celebrating a birthday. The word celebrate is not exactly the term I would use. What I saw was a little disconcerting, but it was something common I remember from my youth.

Most of the adults were hunched over; not just the old ones. Their heads were hanging low. The corners of their mouths were permanently pointing downwards. There was heaviness upon all of them. Their steps were painful, like the gravity around them was more powerful. All of the ladies had the same look about them; long dresses that covered everything, long hair and no make-up. (I am not saying that dressing like this is wrong, I'm simply telling you what I saw.)

They looked like the "obey God or else" crowd that I grew up with. Some of them had ailments that you could physically see. One had an oxygen tank. One had a walker and was struggling. One had physical deformities. Some of the others just looked like they were in pain.

The younger children looked exactly like the older ones. It's like they had a cloning machine somewhere. Some of the children had visible physical ailments as well. One of the girls had a hard plastic brace that she wore around her chest and back. I got the impression that there was a spirit of infirmity among them and they were clueless of it.

That is what I remember growing up with. I belonged to churches just like that. The patriarchs of those churches had whole families with debilitating ailments, sickness and, at times, physical deformities. The only well and healthy people were new converts. Everyone who had been there for any length of time had developed some sort of health problem.

On Testimony Night, it seemed like the older the saint was, the more Job-like the testimonies became. Listening to them talk, one by one, you would get the impression that they believed God had put those infirmities upon them. They would then talk about Heaven like it was their only hope. (Job did that as well in chapter 19.) It was really quite depressing, but if it is what you grew up with and what you are used to, you don't notice the heaviness.

It's a lot like those weight loss shows where someone loses 80 pounds and then straps 80 pounds of weight around their body and tries to walk with it. When it was on them all the time when they were overweight, they were used to it. But, when they were free of it, they were burdened by it when they strapped that weight back on. I will never get back under that spiritual heaviness ever again!

I hope you'll break free and say the same thing by the end of this book as well.

Chapter 6: *The Second Wave*

Now There Was A Day Again, Again

Job 2:1-3 (HCSB) *"Again there was a day when the sons of God came to present themselves before the Lord, and Satan also came among them to present himself before the Lord. . . ."*

Here we go again. There's that "there was a day when" again. So, after the smoke cleared and everything settled down, Satan waited for the response that he wanted. He waited and waited, but never got it. So what does he do? The same thing he did the last time. He tried the exact same thing again and, wouldn't you know it, got the exact same result.   What was the point in that? He knew God would see him again. I think it is kind of funny that God had to point him out yet again. You would think that the angels would have figured it out on their own this time. Satan is quite the master of disguise. Don't ever forget that. Even if you figure out his disguise, he is so good at it that he will most likely fool you again with the same disguise. He does it all the time.

We see in this second meeting that the dialogue is about the same, but God says to Satan concerning Job in verse 3,

**". . . and he (Job) *still holds fast his integrity, although you incited Me against him to ruin him without cause."*

God never liked the arrangement in the first place. I have heard it taught that God was ok with the idea of Job being tested to prove his integrity. That is not true because God says it was "**without cause**". The only reason that God allowed it to happen is because, legally speaking, His hands were tied in the matter. It displeased and grieved God greatly.

Job 2:4-6 (HCSB), *"Satan answered the Lord and said, 'Skin for skin! Yes, all that a man has he*

will give for his life. However, put forth Your hand now, and touch his bone and his flesh; he will curse You to Your face.' So the Lord said to Satan, 'Behold, he is in your power, only spare his life.' Then Satan went out from the presence of the Lord and smote Job with sore boils from the sole of his foot to the crown on his head."

I love this passage! Seriously, I do! The reason is that it breaks apart a lie of the enemy that many have used to say that God brought Job these calamities. Satan may have said, "Put forth Your hand now, and touch his bone and his flesh." **But, God said, "Behold, he is in your (Satan's) power, only spare his life."** And then SATAN went out and smote Job, **NOT GOD**.

Even in Satan's dialogue with God, he was twisting the truth by saying that God would bring the calamity when Satan was the one that did it. That is how twisted Satan is. Even in God's presence of light and glory where nothing is hidden, Satan was putting a spin on the tale before it even happened. He wanted it recorded that it was God's fault. That is a very powerful truth!

Here is a profound statement: You cannot get Biblical Doctrine from the mouth of Satan. And yet, so many believers have done just that. SATAN is the one that said that God brought destruction on Job, and yet we have whole sects and denominations in the church that preach it as truth!

In John 8:44 (NKJV) Jesus says to the Pharisees concerning Satan,

"You are of your father the devil, and the desires of your father you want to do. He was a murderer from the beginning, and does not stand in the truth, because there is no truth in him. When he speaks a lie, he speaks from his own resources, for he is a liar and the father of it."

Satan is a liar and the truth is not in him. THE TRUTH IS NOT IN HIM! So if there is no truth in him, why are so many quoting what the devil said as Divine Truth?

God did not bring any destruction, sickness or death on Job. None of it was from God. The only thing God did, for legality's sake, was remove His protection. That's it.

Now, let's see what happens when Satan leaves the presence of the Lord the second time.

Job 2:7 (HCSB) *"So, Satan left the Lord's presence and infected Job with incurable boils from the sole of his foot to the top of his head. Then Job took a piece of broken pottery to scrape himself while he sat among the ashes."*

Satan didn't waste any time here. We don't see "now there was a day when". He went straight from God's presence to afflict Job. He was fuming mad and didn't stop to think of some grand scheme like he did the first time. There were no gathering of the generals, no plans and no test runs. This time it appears that Satan just wanted to stick it to Job. It was as if Satan took it personally. I could just see Satan losing his cool with this. The first attack, he was calm, cool and collected. His actions were methodically planned out and precise. What he did was a gruesome work of art. The second attack was more like a childish tantrum. He knew he had failed miserably and he was going to make Job pay for it. Just look at the difference here. The first attack was from a decorated war veteran. The second attack was from a humiliated bully. He just wanted to knock the wind out of Job, give him a black eye and stuff him in a locker.

So, based on this character issue with Satan, you can judge by his attack if it is his first attempt at messing with you in an area, or if he tried, failed and now has come back to throw a tantrum. How about that?

Why No Twenty Questions?

How terrible, and yet Job is still not even raising a single question as to why this happened to him. For crying out loud! The most sane and logical thing to do when something like this happens is to at least ask questions. One comes to mind here: *Why, God?* Here are a few others that would make sense in this situation: *What did I do to bring this upon myself? Who was responsible for this? Where did this come from? Where are You, God?* ETC. God expects you to ask questions. He already knows what is in your heart. You might as well get it out so it doesn't fester.

You know, Job had many exit doors out of this mess, but he chose to ignore every single one of them. He just plodded along and accepted everything that happened as being from God. I just want to enter the story, grab Job by the collar of his robe, and shake him. Maybe a couple slaps while saying, "Wake up!" or "Snap out of it!" might have helped. I'm sure his wife would have loved to have done it if she could have gotten away with it. I could just see her saying, "Wrong answer!" That is kind of what she was doing which we will find out in a minute. Mrs. Job adds insult to injury, but I don't think that is what she was trying to do in this situation at all. Let's take a look at what she says in the next chapter.

Chapter 7: *Job's Wife's Wisdom*

Totally Misunderstood

Job 2:9 (HCSB) *"His wife said to him, "Do you still retain your integrity? Curse your God and die!"*

Wait a minute. So, Satan took all of his children, his livestock, his land, his family business, his political influence, his reputation, his house and his health, but he left the nagging wife untouched? I'm kidding! Actually, I think this woman might just be the sanest and wisest person in the Book of Job. Her momma didn't raise no fool. She is the only one who used deductive reasoning in this whole fiasco.

Confused? Let me put it this way. I do not think she could wrap her brain or her heart around the fact that Job still served the God that supposedly stole, killed and destroyed everything in their lives. This brings up a rather good point. This may be one of the reasons why the conversion rate is so low in the churches that preach this bad doctrine. Who wants to give their life to a God who plans on destroying them some time later after they are converted? That is a rather harsh way of putting it, but I believe that is what it boils down to.

This is a prime example of one of the reasons wives are called helpmeets. We men can be so bull headed in our quests that we shut down the part of our brains that has simple reasoning and logic. We get tunnel vision. Many times, if it weren't for women saying something like, "Are you nuts?! Wait a minute! Stop and think!" us men would head straight to our demise.

Job may have rebuked his wife for what she said, but he later took her advice which was a good thing. That's right. I said it was a good thing. I'm not saying that Job cursing God was a good thing. What I am saying is that his bullheaded piety was not letting him be honest about his situation and his true feelings about his God. He may not have cursed God before she said that, but he spent about 30 or so chapters afterwards confronting God and getting upset and stomping his feet and shaking his fist and lamenting and demanding justice and claiming to have greater righteousness than God and throwing wrong accusations at God and, believe it or not, that was the best thing he could have ever done. So many times our piety and devotion gets in the way of our deliverance. Read that last line again. Once in a while we have to get a little angry and stomp around.

The Almost Audible Voice

I was so messed up while I was a student at Bible College. Every morning, with the exception of Wednesdays, we had Chapel worship service at 8 in the morning. That was my favorite part of the day. During one semester, I spent every service crying out to God. I used to say, "Be real to me, God! Be real to me, God! Reveal Yourself to me! Be real to me!" I wanted God to move upon my life and I was crying out constantly to no avail until one day He spoke back to me in an almost audible voice. He said, "You first!"

This stirred me to anger, which is exactly what God was trying to do. You see, I had been so pious and religious in my crying out that it kept me from being honest with God. I had mentioned to you before that I grew up thinking that God hated me. I was getting free of that lie little by little, but something had developed in me over the years that was so deep and hidden in the shadows of my heart. I actually hated God in some ways. I hated Him for hating me. I hated him for all the character flaws I pinned on Him that came from my own not so perfect relationship with my own father.

My heart was cold, but I cleverly hid it with piety and devotion. When God said, "You first", it opened up the floodgates of rage, and for the first time in my life, I opened up my stone cold heart and let the bats out.

I dropped my hands down and said, "Well, for starters, You certainly ruined a good worship service!" (I will cover idolatry and worshiping worship in a later chapter.) And then I began pouring out accusations at God, and for the next couple of months, I laid it on

Him! I said, "I hate You for this! I hate You for that! How dare You do this and that!" And for some things, I actually had to write them down before I could say them. They were too terrible to just say out loud. I had no idea all that ugly was inside me. It was bad!

I had deceived my own heart for a very long time. When I finally came to the end of my railing, I said, "God, I hate You! But I don't want to hate You!" He then said to me, "Finally! Now I can be real to You!" After that, He swept into my life in such a powerful way and moved upon me so mightily! It was awesome! He did such a powerful work in me in that season, and at the end of it I was a different person.

The point here is that God does not respond to devotion and piety if it is void of honesty and transparency. You will see this later in Job's story. That is why King David was regarded so highly with his love for God. He was always honest, open and transparent with God. If you don't believe me, read through all of the Psalms. They are an emotional rollercoaster of pain, sorrow, joy and elation. David held nothing back from God. David had no illusions about himself – he poured out everything that he was to God, the good, the bad, and the ugly. Before we get there we have to go back to Job's wife.

The Thing About Glaciers

Another thing that is happening with Mrs. Job's only statement here is that she is pointing out a HUGE character flaw with Job. There is a commonality found in the layout of the Book of Job, and that is how the author will give us a glimpse at the beginning of the story that will later become a much larger issue later in the story. It is like looking at a glacier. You don't know the size of it until you submerge deep into the water. That is what happens in this story over and over again.

When Mrs. Job says, "Still holding fast to that integrity of yours . . ." what we see here is the author showing us the top part of the glacier. Then we submerge and see the overwhelming size of it.

One of Job's biggest issues was of him trying to keep a spotless reputation in his community. He was so concerned about his name in the community. He had an unhealthy obsession with everyone seeing him as an upright man who was blameless. Typical Politician. He worked hard on it for years. We will see later that even in his impoverished state, he was desperately trying to retain his image as one who is blameless and upright. It is so bad that he forgets what really matters. And what really mattered? She was standing right in front of him.

The Real Victim

One huge fact we have to take into account with Mrs. Job (I wish we knew her name.) is that she was also one who lost everything. She lost all of her babies; the children she brought into the world. In her day that was how women obtained status. Of course, we assume she loved them too, as any mother would.

She lost her home, which was her place of security. She lost her status as "The First Lady" of the most influential man in the region. She lost her wealth; everything they owned of value was destroyed. She lost her strong, upright, leader-in-the-community, loving, caring and supportive husband, and found that she was now married to a useless drama goon who insisted on sitting out in the open in a pile of ashes so that everyone could see him scrape his nasty sore-covered, half-naked, filthy body with a piece of broken pottery. Talk about going from princess to pauper!

She was probably going through greater pain than he was, but she no longer was able to collapse into his strong arms. She was, probably for the first time in her life, truly alone. In her day and in that culture, there was no escaping this delightful reality of hers unless her husband passed on. She was stuck with him. If he were to curse God and finally be struck down for good, she could go back home to her parents and try to begin rebuilding her shattered life.

Job was so focused on retaining his image and integrity and making sure he didn't slip up or mess up after this calamity happened that he neglected his wife. She was in pain, and what was Job doing? He was lifting his hands in a pious public show of "worship" saying, "Blessed be the Name of the Lord" trying to keep up an appearance that he was unshaken by the tragedy when he should have been comforting his poor wife. We don't see anywhere that Job tried to comfort his grieving wife. That is a tragedy within a tragedy. I will say it again. Typical Politician.

I'm sure she was also mad at Job for serving such a terrible God who turned on them in spite of Job's life of integrity and uprightness. How could she not be? Job's bad choice of who to worship was what brought this calamity in the first place, or so she thought.

Also notice that she said, "Curse *your* God. . ." She didn't claim ownership of Job's God. She wasn't in agreement with Job's choice of worship. I'm sure she had gods of her own she believed in before her husband introduced her to his God. When life was good and they were blessed, I doubt she had any problems with Job's choice or his prayers and sacrifices. But when everything was suddenly gone, and Job himself was blaming God with his, "The Lord gives and the Lord takes away," I don't know that her faith in Job's God was enough to withstand the storm.

The reason isn't said, but I deduce that she said "your God" because she either abandoned her faith after this or secretly never put her faith in Job's God in the first place. How horrible to trust in your husband's faith and uprightness to appease his God and keep you and your family safe and sound only to find out it wasn't enough after all. Talk about feeling betrayed.

Another thing you have to see is that when she said, "Still holding fast to that integrity of yours? Curse your God and die" she may have been mocking his flawed doctrine. You can count on a wife to mock you when your unbridled bullheadedness gets you into a mess. It was the, "See, I told you so!" thing to do. I believe that she knew there was something screwy about his beliefs. She probably even tried to confront him about it, and now, after the world they knew had crashed and burned, she is very bitterly pointing it out to him.

I believe it is unfair that Job's wife is the character most criticized by the church in this story. Put yourself in her shoes for a day and see how you handle losing all your children to a natural disaster, losing all of your livestock, hired hands, wealth, home and status in the community and are supposedly completely betrayed by the God you and your family have chosen to worship. Then imagine that after everything else, the last bit of your life you still possess, your husband, is stricken with incurable boils and instead of DOING something about *anything*, he sits like a lump on a log scraping himself with one of your broken dishes! AND he is completely ignoring you. I think she handled things pretty well for the lot she was dealt.

> **Job 2:10 (HCSB)** *"'You speak as a foolish woman speaks,' he told her. 'Should we accept only good from God and not adversity?' Throughout all this Job did not sin in what he said."*

The part that I can't wrap my brain around is, "Throughout all this Job did not sin in what he said." Well, he may not have cursed God, but he certainly cursed and dishonored his poor grieving wife. Someone else had to have heard Job say this to her for it to have been recorded in this story. He was the most influential man of his day. I am sure everyone at all times was in his business looking for him to fail.

Let me make this real to you. If it happened today, there would have been news reporters with video cameras surrounding Job and his wife like a swarm of bees in front of the smoldering remains of their estate. News choppers would be flying overhead. The Police Department, Crime Scene Investigators and maybe the FBI would be there investigating with yellow tape and barriers set up. There would be the "Haters" with their protest signs, gloating over his loss. Everyone from the town would be there with their iPhones and Androids out capturing what they saw. With all the microphones in

Job's face, Job was asked to give a statement about what happened. And, as we have seen, he was trying to keep up an appearance of a blameless and upright man, unshaken, who is still approved of by God as the man of the hour.

Out of all the things he could have said, like "No comment" or "I don't know how we are going to get through this" or "The pain we feel is just too overwhelming" or "We need some time to ourselves for a while to work through this. It just doesn't seem real", he chose to say, "The Lord gives and the Lord takes away. Blessed be the Name of the Lord." He probably said it with the Pentecostal quiver in his voice with his arms raised.

This was the anvil that broke the camel's back. Mrs. Job finally had enough and interrupted in a moment mixed with feelings of absolute rage, pain, betrayal and sorrow, she, with a tear stained face, bellows out, "Still holding fast to that integrity of yours? Why don't you curse your God and die!"

Instead of responding rightly to his poor wife who was completely overcome with grief and hopelessness, in front of the whole town, and quickly escorting her away from the scene to comfort her, Job stayed completely in character and did the worst possible thing he could have done. He belittles her and dishonors her in front of everyone by calling her a foolish woman and then gives her a quick Bible lesson explaining why she should not be grieving over the loss of her children, status, wealth, etcetera in their lives. What a jerk!

Like I said, Job's wife was very much alone.

In the next chapter we jump forward to Job's response to God after the second calamity strikes.

Chapter 8: *The Wicked Mob Boss*

Job And His Swearing Problem

Job 3:1-6 (HCSB) *"After this Job began to speak and cursed the day he was born. He said, 'May the day I was born perish, and the night when they said 'A boy is conceived.' If only that day had turned to darkness! May God above not care about it, or light shine on it. May darkness and gloom reclaim it, and a cloud settle over it. May an eclipse of the sun terrify it. If only darkness had taken that night away! May it not appear among the days of the year or to be listed in the calendar.'"*

Oh, for heaven's sake! May the blackest black blackness blacken out the sun with black-like blackish blackness black enough to blacken out the day and make it black as black! That's not all. If you want to torture yourself, read the next 30 or so chapters, or just take a hot poker and gouge out your eye balls because that is what you will want to do after reading it. No wonder his friends said things like, "How long until you stop talking?" There are 30 chapters of it!

There is only one other person in the Bible who comes close to lamenting as gut wrenching as Job. That would be Jeremiah. The only reason that he comes close is because Jeremiah is quoting Job. He actually takes it a little deeper into the dungeon of despair, but I won't give him the credit because he started off by loosely quoting Job. Job wins this one hands down. Well, I wouldn't call it winning exactly. Let's read it:

Jeremiah 22:14-15 (HCSB) *"Cursed be the day on which I was born. The day my mother bore me – let it never be blessed. Cursed be the man who brought the news to my father, saying, 'A male child is born to you,' bringing him great joy. Let that man* *be like the cities the Lord overthrew without compassion. Let him hear an outcry in the morning and a war cry at noontime because he didn't kill me in the womb so that my mother might have been my grave, her womb eternally pregnant. Why did I come out of the womb to see only struggle and sorrow, to end my life in shame?"*

I think his mother would have a problem with the idea of being eternally pregnant. I think most women would have a problem with the idea of being eternally pregnant. I think most men would have a problem with the idea of their wives being eternally pregnant. Anyway, someone should give Jeremiah a guitar, skinny jeans and some eyeliner. He could start a band. He could call it, "Eternally Pregnant." Such drama!

There is a good reason why Jeremiah's version was a little more disparaging. When you are suffering from a bitter experience, one of the worst things you can do is find something bitter to associate with, like Jeremiah did. It is like when the love of your life dumps you and you get 5 tubs of Ben & Jerry's Ice Cream and gorge yourself while watching a Romance Movie Marathon on the Lifetime or Hallmark Channels with some country love songs playing softly in the background. By the end of it, you are sobbing hysterically while shoveling as fast as you can heaping spoonful after spoonful of ice-cream to try to medicate the pain when all you are doing is multiplying it exponentially. It's actually quite comical to see someone else doing it, though. Now, imagine Job or Jeremiah saying what they said while eating 5 tubs of ice cream with tears streaming down their faces. (Yes, I think I took that a little far.)

The only reason I can joke about this is because I have been in that place more than a few times. I was not as gracious as Job and Jeremiah were. There was a lot more swearing involved. I did, however, make sure that no one was around to hear me say it to record it. I like attention and all, but apparently not as much as Job and Jeremiah. Let's get back to what I was saying about Job. There are 30 chapters of it!

Lucky for you, I pulled out some of the best of the best, or should I say the worst of the worst, that Job said. You might need to sit down to read these. It starts off kind of light and then it gets really insufferable. It's like a Shakespeare Tragedy with a steroid overdose. I address each thing Job says about God with a rebuttal and some will have a scripture or two to help us determine if Job spoke out of ignorance or wisdom.

Job's "Heavenly Platitudes"

9:13, *"God does not hold back His anger."*

There are many places in the Old Testament where it says, "and the anger of the Lord was kindled", but each time the anger of the Lord was kindled, He exercised patience and long suffering with His people. He always held back His anger to give whoever caused it a chance to change their ways. If God does not hold back His anger, then Jesus would have never come in the flesh. If God does not hold back His anger, then He never would have sent His prophets to warn the Israelites of destruction for hundreds of years before He actually did anything. If God does not hold back His anger, then the Israelites would never have returned alive from their exile in Babylon. If God does not hold back His anger, then the Israelites would have never been given 40 years to get their act straight before getting another chance to enter the Promised Land. If God does not hold back His anger, then He would never have told Noah to build an ark for 120 years and would have completely wiped out humanity with the flood. If God does not hold back His anger, then Adam and Eve would have never made it out of the Garden of Eden alive. So, no, Job had it wrong. And even if Job was right about God's anger, he would have been wrong about where God was directing it. God was not angry with Job. Moving on.

Job 9:16-20, *"If I summoned Him and He answered me, I do not believe He would pay*

attention to what I said. He batters me with a whirlwind, and multiplies my wounds without cause. He doesn't let me catch my breath, but soaks me with bitter experiences."

Job just told on himself. Let's break this down. *"If I summoned Him. . ."* His first mistake in dealing with this was that he DIDN'T summon God. That should always be our first response; even if it's a "why God". Always call on God first. He always has the best solution.

". . . and He answered me. . ." Job is saying it without saying it "if" rather than "when". This leads me to believe that he has never actually called on God. If he had called on God at any time in His life, God would have been faithful to answer.

"I do not believe He would pay attention to what I said." How do you know that if you won't even summon Him? The first thing you should do in every situation is SUMMON GOD. The second thing you should do is WAIT FOR AN ANSWER. Most of your relationship with God is through PRAYER. So, we can almost safely say that Job was not a man of prayer. That's scary! Here is a truth that you can glean from this. Lack of prayer leads way to assumption. When you see someone making accusations at God assuming that He will or won't do this or that, you can bet that they are not one who is given to prayer.

Back to Job's ridiculous assumption about God, we see from the conversations between God and Satan, that it was Satan that battered him with a whirlwind, and Satan who multiplied his wounds without cause. It was Satan who wouldn't let him catch his breath, and it was Satan who soaked him with bitter experiences. Yet Job lays every bit of the blame on God.

How often have we been caught doing that very thing? I know that I have been the guilty party in this many times. It sounds to me like Job knew the voice of the enemy better than he knew the voice of God. That is true with many believers. They account the bitter condemnation from the mouth of the enemy to be the conviction of the Holy Spirit. In John 16:8-11 we see whom the Holy Spirit really convicts and of what.

>*"And when He* (The Holy Spirit) *has come, He will convict the world of sin, and of righteousness, and of judgment: of sin, because they do not believe in Me; of righteousness, because I go to My Father and you see Me no more; of judgment, because the ruler of this world is judged."*

So we see that He convicts the unsaved because of sin, which draws them to God. We see that He convicts the world of judgment because Satan is judged. Here comes the best part! He convicts his disciples of RIGHTEOUSNESS! Not of unrighteousness. He convicts us that we who are in Christ are rendered righteous! There is therefore now NO condemnation for those who are in Christ Jesus! Condemnation is uttered from the mouth of the enemy; not God. A good habit to get into is learning to decipher the difference between condemnation and conviction.

Back to Job's bitter accusation, not one place in the Old or the New Testament do we see God battering someone and wounding them without cause. What is amazing is that God does show up near the end in a whirlwind, but it is right before He restores everything to Job. Satan's whirlwind destroys and brings chaos, while God's whirlwind brings restoration, life and order.

>**Job 9:22, *"Therefore I say, 'He destroys both the blameless and the wicked.'"***

Scripture says something completely opposite. In Matthew 5:45 Jesus says,

>*"For He causes His sun to rise on the evil and the good, and sends rain on the righteous and the unrighteous."*

The sun and the rain are both symbolic of God's blessing. I've noticed that in our technologically advanced "space age" culture that rain is considered a lot of times more of a bad thing than a good thing. We have to remember that those who penned the Scriptures were not

21st Century, car driving, 9 to 5 working, weekend loving, grocery shopping westerners who thought rain was an inconvenience that kept them from entertainment venues, but rather simple farming folk who depended on the rain for their very livelihood.

Rain, in Biblical days and most other parts of the world, is considered a blessing from God. So when it says, *"and sends rain on the righteous and the unrighteous"* it means that God sends His blessing on both the righteous and the unrighteous. Why? It is because God is a good God. God blesses both the blameless and the wicked, but Job said the exact opposite. Moving on.

Job 9:23, *"When disaster brings sudden death, He mocks the despair of the innocent. The earth is handed over to the wicked. He blindfolds its judges."*

Here is a good counter scripture –

Psalm 89:14 (HCSB) *"Righteousness and Justice are the foundation of Your Throne; faithful love and truth go before You."*

God's foundation is righteousness and justice, and He is encompassed around with faithful love and truth. Mocking the despair of the innocent is not justice, not righteous, absent of love and void of truth. What Job said goes completely against scripture and against the very nature of God. If that is not enough:

1st Corinthians 13:6 *"Love finds no joy in unrighteousness, but rejoices in the truth."*

We know that God is love personified, so He finds no joy in unrighteousness and he rejoices in the truth. God tells us to protect the innocent and He would not tell us to do that if He wasn't already doing that Himself. Remember that God does not live by a double standard.

Job 9:30-31, *"If I wash myself with snow and cleanse my hands with lye, then You dip me in a pit of mud and my own clothes despise me!"*

This is also completely opposite of the character and nature of God. It should read, "If I am in a pit of mud and despised by my own clothes, then you wash me white as snow and cleanse my hands with lye."

This goes against the very nature of God. This goes against all of the countless stories in the Word of God where mankind came to God with their unrighteousness and He made them clean. It has never been the other way around. NEVER. It is truly amazing how Job had it so backwards. He did not know God at all. He may have offered up worship unto God, but he was completely clueless as to who He was and what He was like. Again, all of this is one of the symptoms of a man not praying.

What is sad is that I could say this about myself at one time. I was offering up worship to a God I didn't know. Job even admits that he didn't know God at the end of the Book of Job, but we will get into that later.

Job 9:34, *"Let Him take His rod away from me so His terror will no longer frighten me."*

There's that terror (yare H3372) again. It's amazing how much of a stronghold it had in Job's life. And we should know by now that Job didn't just become fearful of God on his own. Satan was at work the whole time messing with Job's psyche until he had him terrified enough that Satan could go to God with an accusation.

And concerning this "rod" that Job mentions, we see in the Psalms that God's Rod and Staff are used for comfort and correction, not for fear and destruction.

Job 10:2, *"Do not declare me guilty! Let me know why You prosecute me."*

While this may be a perfectly logical question for Job to ask God, and I applaud Job for finally asking questions, we have already learned that Job was not on trial. God was not prosecuting Job. Satan was the prosecutor here. This calamity, in God's eyes, was without cause.

Satan still lies to us in this way. I have even heard it said many times by men and women of God that Jesus is interceding on our behalf to keep the Father calmed down enough to not strike us or declare us guilty. Then the passage about Jesus being our intercessor is used where He is praying for us to keep us from being squished by Father God.

First of all, the term intercessor used means to stand in or bridge a gap. What bridged the gap between God and man? THE CROSS. And if the Father really felt that way about us, He never would have sent His Son to die for our sins. The Father, Son and Holy Spirit are One and are not in disagreement. It is not a "Good Cop, Bad Cop" relationship that I have seen portrayed in many sermons.

Jesus said, "I and the Father are One. If you've seen Me, you've seen the Father." God is not schizophrenic. And my last point in this before I move on is that the Cross was not needed because God the Father was angry. The Cross was needed because, from a legal standpoint, we were found guilty in God's righteous court and God wanted to redeem us and make us His own again. In order to do that, justice had to be served. And since we couldn't pay our debt, out of His great rampant love for humanity, He chose to take our place. He paid the ultimate price.

Greater love has no man than this; that he should lay his life down for his friends. I don't see how you could possibly fit anger anywhere into that equation. God has never been the prosecutor or accuser. We all know who has that role.

Job 10:3, *"Is it good for You to oppress, to reject the work of Your hands, and favor the plans of the wicked?"*

Now he is getting insolent in his ranting. You see, none of the questions Job are asking are helping his case. The question above is actually a trap he set for God. It may be a yes or no question, but to answer it in any way means that God is guilty of oppressing and rejecting the work of His hands and favoring the plans of the wicked, which He is not.

Again, God does not oppress. He is not known as The Oppressor anywhere in the Word of God. He is known as The Deliverer, The Redeemer and The Savior. Nowhere do we see God rejecting the work of His hands, and nowhere do we see Him favoring the plans of the wicked.

> **Job 10:13, "*Yet You concealed these thoughts in Your heart, I know that this was Your hidden plan!*"**

Now he is claiming to know the thoughts and ways of God; that God had hidden plans. In the Old Testament it was declared by God, Isaiah 55:8:

> **"*'For My thoughts are not your thoughts, and your ways are not my ways.' This is the Lord's declaration. 'For as heaven is higher than the earth, so My ways are higher than your ways, and My thoughts than your thoughts.*"**

There is a time in scripture where we begin to know the thoughts and ways of God. That is when we become redeemed and have the Mind of Christ. And the more and more the Mind of Christ is developed in us, the less and less we give thought to making such accusations at God like Job has.

> **Job 10:17, "*You produce new witnesses against me and multiply Your anger toward me.*"**

Here, Job is saying that God brought his three friends as witnesses against him. They may have been witnesses against him, but it had nothing to do with God. They themselves were idolatrous and did not know God.

> **Job 12:6, "*The tents of robbers are safe and those who provoke God are secure; God's power provides this.*"**

Now Job is contradicting himself. Previously he said, *"He destroys both the blameless and the wicked."* Now he is saying that God protects the wicked with His power. Nowhere in scripture do we see this to be true.

Before I go further, I must point out how much of what he is saying appears to be coming from his past observations. He believes he has seen God protect, enable and favor the plans of the wicked on a regular basis. It's as if he had been observing God do these things the whole time. For that to happen, bitterness would have had to have been in his heart long before the enemy rained down destruction upon him. He was bitter and filtered everything he saw through his bitterness filter. The destruction that ensued just proved to him what he had already believed. I'm going to have you reread some of what he said so that you will see it.

"He destroys both the blameless and the wicked."

"When disaster brings sudden death, He mocks the despair of the innocent."

"The earth is handed over to the wicked. He blindfolds its judges."

"Is it good for You to oppress, to reject the work of Your hands, and favor the plans of the wicked?"

"The tents of robbers are safe and those who provoke God are secure; God's power provides this."

These are all things that he is convinced of and that apparently had been in his heart the whole time. He wasn't just afraid that God would destroy his children for their bad behavior. He believed secretly that God was unjust, unfair and diabolical. Because of this, he already had a seed of bitterness that was growing in his heart. What kept him from addressing this bitterness was the fear of loss. When the fear of losing everything was gone (because he lost everything) he no longer had a good enough reason to hide his bitterness.

His terrible fear of God kept him from showing how he really felt about the situation when the first wave of destruction hit. But don't think for a minute that his children or his wife were oblivious to what he secretly believed the whole time. It could be why his children didn't follow him in his faith. Children can tell when their parents are fake. Bitterness and fear are very visible on the outside, and there is not much you can do to disguise it. Job's wife knew this. She knew he was bitter and afraid, but was wearing a mask, hence the phrase "Still holding fast to your 'integrity'? Curse your God and die." You are the only one who is really fooled by your mask.

Job 13:24, "*Why do You hide Your face and consider me Your enemy?*"

God spends all of His time defending Job and declaring him blameless and upright. He even shows up in a whirlwind and rebukes Job's friends and declares Job to be blameless and upright. God does not consider Job to be his enemy. I would even say that Job, in the end, gets special treatment from God when God himself shows up in a whirlwind to defend Job. Who else can claim this?

Job 14:19, "*As water wears away stones and torrents from the Land, so You destroy a man's hope.*"

Hey, put THAT in a worship song! No, please don't. Actually, according to Jeremiah, the Lord has plans to prosper us, and give us a future filled with hope, not to destroy our hope.

Job 16:7-14, "*Surely He has now exhausted me. You have devastated my entire family. You have shriveled me up – it has become a witness; my frailty rises up against me and testifies to my face. His anger tears at me and He harasses me. He gnashes His teeth at me. My enemy pierces me with His eyes. They open their mouths against me and strike my cheeks with contempt; they join themselves together against me. God hands me over to unjust men; He throws me into the hands of the wicked. I was at ease, but He shattered me; He seized me by the scruff of the neck and smashed me to pieces. He set me up as a target; His archers surround me. He pierces my kidneys without mercy and pours my bile on the ground. He breaks*"

*through my defenses again and again; He charges
at me like a warrior."*

If we didn't know this was Job talking about God, we would think that the monolog given was about Satan. Satan devastates. Satan tears at and harasses. Satan testifies against us. Satan hands us over to unjust men. Satan throws us into the hands of the wicked. (or he would really like to) Goodness! These are character traits of Satan and yet Job said this about God. He calls God his enemy.

This one is too overwhelming. I don't think I need to rebut it because it does a good job of it on its own. The pain that was in Job's heart must have been crushing! To think that God is against you and has destroyed you and everything around you because of an intense seething hatred of you is too terrifying to even think about. No wonder he spends 30 chapters releasing a torrential catharsis of pain!

If he were in New Testament times, I would even say that he would need to have a time of deliverance ministry given to him. If God could show us Job at that time with our spiritual eyes opened, we would probably see a horde of demons and harassing spirits surrounding and pummeling Job mercilessly. I cannot imagine the pressure that was on him. It makes me thank God for the spiritual authority we have in Christ to command the enemy to flee from us.

**Job 19:6, *"Then understand that it is God who
has wronged me and caught me in His net."***

God does not set up snares and traps, Psalms tells us that He delivers us from the snare of the fowler and sends His angels to guard our feet. Satan sets up ambushes, traps, snares and nets for mankind to stumble upon.

**Job 19:21, *"Have mercy on me, my friends;
have mercy, for God's hand has struck me."***

It sounds like a Psalm of David, but BACKWARDS! If King David had said it, it would have sounded like, "Have mercy on me, my God, have mercy, for my enemy's hand has struck me!" But we see that Job confused his Friend for his enemy and his enemies for his friends.

Job 21:19, *"God reserves a person's punishment for his children."*

Here is another contradicting statement of Job's. Job, a blameless and upright man, continually made sacrifices for his children so that God would not strike them for any wickedness in their hearts. The thing he feared was that God would take out his family for their sins, and now he has changed his story a little. Now he is saying that God punished his children for his sins instead of punishing him. He seems to be throwing every bit of mud that he can find at God.

Looking at all of this, I believe it is safe to say that Job really wasn't grounded in any sort of belief system concerning Jehovah, but was mostly motivated by fear. That sounds like some churches I have been a part of when I was growing up. The foundation was never clear, but fear was what determined everything. Thank You, Lord, for showing me Your love which cast out that fear! Hallelujah! Thank God that He is not known as The Punisher.

Job 27:2, *"As God lives, who has deprived me of justice, and the Almighty who has made me bitter. . ."*

This is his crowning statement on it all. This sums it all up. Job thought that God was unjust and full of uncontrollable rage and hatred. He also said that the Almighty made him bitter. And as we saw earlier, Job was already bitter before the destruction came. And when we harbor bitterness in our hearts, it clouds our view of God and His grace. And bitterness produces more bitterness, which produces more bitterness. Bitterness is another trap that ties God's hands. Bitterness is one of Satan's greatest weapons he uses to dismantle our faith. A great book that I would like to recommend on this issue is "The Bait Of Satan" by John Bevere. It is a must read for those who struggle with bitterness.

I've got one more thing he said that I want to address, but first I want to let you read from beginning to end all that he said together. Let it sink in. The surety of your foundation doesn't become apparent until you find yourself in a sticky predicament. It is then that what was in your heart from the beginning comes out. It is then that the world sees your true colors. The same can be said about Job. Let's do a recap of what he said. This is going to make you sick:

"God does not hold back His anger. If I summoned Him and He answered me, I do not believe He would pay attention to what I said. He batters me with a whirlwind, and multiplies my wounds without cause. He doesn't let me catch my breath, but soaks me with bitter experiences.

Therefore I say, 'He destroys both the blameless and the wicked.' When disaster brings sudden death, He mocks the despair of the innocent. The earth is handed over to the wicked. He blindfolds its judges.

If I wash myself with snow and cleanse my hands with lye, then You dip me in a pit of mud and my own clothes despise me! Let Him take His rod away from me so His terror will no longer frighten me. Do not declare me guilty! Let me know why You prosecute me.

Is it good for You to oppress, to reject the work of Your hands, and favor the plans of the wicked? Yet You concealed these thoughts in Your heart, I know that this was Your hidden plan!

You produce new witnesses against me and multiply Your anger toward me. The tents of robbers are safe and those who provoke God are secure; God's power provides this.

Why do You hide Your face and consider me Your enemy? As water wears away stones and torrents from the Land, so You destroy a man's hope. Surely He has now exhausted me. You have devastated my entire family. You have shriveled me up – it has become a witness; my frailty rises up against me and testifies to my face. His anger tears at me and He harasses me. He gnashes His teeth at me. My enemy pierces me with His eyes. They open their mouths against me and strike my cheeks with contempt; they join themselves together against me.

God hands me over to unjust men; He throws me into the hands of the wicked. I was at ease, but He shattered me; He seized me by the scruff of the neck and smashed me to pieces. He set me up as a target; His archers surround me. He pierces my kidneys without mercy and pours my bile on the ground. He breaks through my defenses again and again; He charges at me like a warrior.

Then understand that it is God who has wronged me and caught me in His net. Have mercy on me, my friends; have mercy, for God's hand has struck me. God reserves a person's punishment for his children. As God lives, who has deprived me of justice, and the Almighty who has made me bitter..."

I have a question for you: Does this sound anything like the God you love and worship? I hope not!

I actually saved what Job said first for last, 2:21b,

"The Lord gives and the Lord takes away."

Now, we just looked at what was really in Job's heart in the other things Job said. We see that he was not a man of prayer, which led to wild and ridiculous assumptions about God. We now see the foundation of his faith, or maybe I should say the foundation of his fear. How many of us are guilty of this? I'm raising both of my hands here! With those statements placed next to the last quote, it gives a less noble spin to it. With all this brought to light, do you still want to quote this man? If he was here today, would you invite him to speak at your church? Would you hire him to be a grief counselor? I hope not! Let's look at some other passages of scripture.

Romans 11:29 *"Since God's gracious gifts and calling are irrevocable."*

Numbers 23:19 *"God is not a man who lies, or a son of man who changes His mind."*

2nd Corinthians 1:20 (NKJV[9]) *"For all the promises of God in Him are Yes, and in Him Amen, to the glory of God through us."*

John 10:10 *"A thief comes only to steal and to kill and to destroy. I have come that they may have life and have it in abundance."*

Luke 11:11 *"What father among you, if his son asks for a fish, will give him a snake instead of a fish? Or if he asks for an egg, will give him a scorpion? If you then, who are evil, know how to give good gifts to your children, how much more will the heavenly Father give the Holy Spirit to those who ask Him?"*

The Misunderstood Master

Nowhere do we see God take away what He has given to a blameless and faithful man. You ask, "But what about the passage in Matthew 25:28:

'So take the talent from him and give it to the one who has 10 talents. For to everyone who has, more will be given, and he will have more than enough. But from the one who does not have, even what he has will be taken away from him. And throw this good for nothing slave into the outer darkness. In that place there will be weeping and gnashing of teeth.'"

There can be no comparison between the lazy slave and Job, who was the wealthiest man in the land. And this parable, not an actual interaction between Jesus and a lazy slave, is a picture of The End when you stand before God and you give an account of what you had and what you did with it. This man, in the end, had nothing to show for himself and was cast into outer darkness which is a reference of Hell.

---

[9] New King James Version

There is one comparison that we can make, however. Both the lazy slave and Job believed that their Master was wicked and unjust and they were terribly afraid of Him. And both lost everything and it was all their fault, not God's fault. You see, when we have a view of God like they did, it will ultimately, one way or another, bring destruction upon us.

Job was, apparently, not a man in covenant with God. He didn't know God. His perception of God was completely skewed, and we shall see later on that he was rather arrogant and proud as he spewed out all of his accolades to his friends. He declared that he was more righteous and just than God. Why are so many people trying to glean wisdom from this man? You might as well go to Satan, because Job's perception of God was almost as twisted as what Satan will tell you!

Counting It All As Loss

Quoting Job before his encounter with Almighty God is like quoting Paul before he met Jesus on the Road to Damascus, or Peter before he was baptized in the Holy Spirit, or Moses before he saw the Burning Bush, or Jacob before he wrestled with God. Nothing they had to say before they were radically encountered by God was worth paying any attention to. Saul was later renamed Paul. Jacob was later renamed Israel. Simon was later renamed Peter. Abram was later renamed Abraham. Maybe, if Jobab and Job were the same person (as discussed in a previous chapter), Job was renamed Jobab. Regardless, the before and after pictures of Job are completely different. Paul said in Philippians 3:8 concerning all he learned before coming to Christ,

> *"Yet indeed I also count all things loss for the excellence of the knowledge of Christ Jesus my Lord, for whom I have suffered the loss of all things, and count them as rubbish, that I may gain Christ" (NKJV)*

All that we were before our encounter with Almighty God is loss. As the saying goes (in a backwards sort of way), "A man with knowledge is always at the mercy of a man with experience." Job's experience with God laid waste to his knowledge of God.

The phrase, "The Lord gives and the Lord takes away" comes from a very bitter and terrified man who worshipped a God whom he thought was a corrupt, unjust, unrighteous, evil, wicked, rage filled mob boss in the sky who would take pleasure in destroying the innocent without cause. (Again, this sounds like some of the churches I grew up in!) That is where the motivation to say that phrase came from.

It's not a noble, selfless statement of unbridled and wholehearted worship, but rather a misguided, unfairly spoken accusation of a bitter, tormented man towards a completely misunderstood God whom he lived in absolute fear and terror of. Believing that about God was what got him in that situation in the first place. That is why I said in the beginning that it was ironic that it was a universal statement of loss.

If you knew what was best for you, you would never ever utter that statement out of your mouth ever again! A more accurate thing to say is, "The Lord gives and gives and gives and gives and gives and keeps on giving and keeps on giving and never ever relents because He absolutely and unequivocally adores His children with a rampant unconditional love that can never be satisfied! Blessed be the Name of The Lord!"

The only things the Lord has ever taken from you is guilt, punishment, eternal damnation, shame, sin, misery, grief, despair,, hopelessness, sickness, disease, and the list goes on and on. I could end the book on that note, but there is so much more that we can garner from this story. I want to talk about Job's uplifting and encouraging friends Eliphaz, Bildad and Zophar, but first I need to bring Jesus Christ into the picture. Has that ever been done before with the book of Job? Hey! We need to bring SOMEONE into this story who knows what they are talking about!

Chapter 9: Got Compassion?

Our Natural Response

When you see someone who has just lost everything from a natural disaster, what is the first thing that pops into your mind? To a great majority of the world, saved and unsaved, there are thoughts of compassion.

What is the last thing that comes into your mind? Keep in mind it was caused by a natural disaster. The last thing to pop into your mind would be to blame them for it. What would be your thoughts concerning someone who went to a destitute person and, instead of helping that person, blasted them over and over again with blame, guilt and shame relentlessly until they wanted to die? Your answer would either be censored or you would let your foot do the talking for you. Who cares what brought the natural disaster, or what that person's background is, or what religion they are associated with or what they may be guilty of? Where does that come into play with helping your fellow man?

Now, bring it a little closer to home. What if that destitute person was someone who was benevolent in the community; known for repeatedly helping the homeless, the fatherless, the widow and the stranger? Now, bring it close to your heart. What if that person was a close friend of yours? All of this applies to Job as you will see later.

Response and Responsibility

We just discussed the human response. Now, let's discuss responsibility. We as saints have a mandate from the Lord. In the parable of the Sheep and the Goats in Matthew 25:40, Jesus said,

> *"And the King will answer them, 'I assure you:*
> *Whatever you did for one of the least of these*
> *brothers of Mine, you did it for Me.'*

In verse 35 through 36, He lists what was done,

"For I was hungry and you gave Me something to eat; I was thirsty and you gave Me something to drink; I was a stranger and you took Me in; I was naked and you clothed Me; I was sick and you took care of Me; I was in prison and you visited Me."

What is interesting to note is that Job did all of this and more. He was a model saint. He fed the hungry. He took the stranger in. He clothed the naked. He took care of the sick. He was a model citizen. He oozed compassion. We are not so sure that his motives were pure considering the bitterness, self-righteousness and fear he lived with, but he oozed compassion nonetheless. I don't see in the above passage any mention about doctrine, blame, guilt or shame at all.

Let's look at another story in the Gospels.

Luke 10:30-37 *"Jesus took up the question and said: "A man was going down from Jerusalem to Jericho and fell into the hands of robbers. They stripped him, beat him up, and fled, leaving him half dead. A priest happened to be going down that road. When he saw him, he passed by on the other side. In the same way, a Levite, when he arrived at the place and saw him, passed by on the other side. But a Samaritan on the journey came up to him, and when he saw the man, he had compassion. He went over to him and bandaged his wounds, pouring oil and wine. Then he put him on his own animal, brought him to an inn, and took care of him. The next day he took out two denarii, gave them to the innkeeper, and said, "Take care of him. When I come back I'll reimburse you for whatever extra you spend. Which one of these three do you think proved to be a neighbor to the man who fell into the hands of the robbers?" "The one who showed* *mercy to him," they said. Then Jesus told him, "Go and do the same."*

Here's another one:

Luke 16:19-*31* *"There was a rich man who would dress in purple and fine linen, feasting lavishly every day. But a poor man named Lazarus, covered with many sores, was left at his gate. He longed to be filled with what fell from the rich man's table, but instead the dogs would come and lick his sores.*

One day the poor man died and was carried away by the angels to Abraham's side. The rich man also died and was buried. And being in torment in Hades, he looked up and saw Abraham a long way off, with Lazarus at his side. "Father Abraham!" he called out "Have mercy on me and send Lazarus to dip the tip of his finger in water and cool my tongue, because I am in agony in this flame!"

"Son," Abraham said, "Remember that during your life you received your good things, just as Lazarus received bad things, but how he is comforted here, while you are in agony. Besides all of this, a great chasm has been fixed between us and you, so that those who want to pass over from here to you cannot; neither can those from there cross over to us."

"Father, he said, then I beg you to send him to my father's house – because I have five brothers – to warn them, so they won't also come to this place of torment."

But Abraham said, "They have Moses and the prophets; they should listen to them." "No, father Abraham, he said, "But if someone from the dead goes to them, they will repent. But he told him, 'If they don't listen to Moses and the prophets they will not be persuaded if someone rises from the dead."

In all of Christ's Parables, not one of the sick, blind or lame was read the riot act before getting healed. Not one. (Except for the blind man whom the apostles were discussing generational curses over. You see where that got them.) Christ had compassion for all. He had unconditional love for all. So, the proper response when we see someone who has just lost everything, went through a tragedy, or has an incurable disease is to have compassion on them and help them.

Cultural Hindrances

This brings us to another issue concerning culture. In certain religions and cultures, compassion is not allowed as a secondary response. There are a few examples that come to mind here. In the Islamic faith, when calamity falls upon someone, you are not allowed to help them. They believe it was the will of Allah that calamity fell upon that person, so to help them person would be going against the will of Allah. That is why when an earthquake, tsunami, hurricane or other natural disaster happens in the world there are hardly any relief efforts coming from Islamic nations.

There are many religions in India that are the same way. While this practice is now illegal, the caste system is still in place in certain areas where different people are compartmentalized into higher and lower social classes. Wikipedia gives an excellent description of the Indian Caste System:

"The Indian caste system is a system of social stratification and social restriction in India in which communities are defined by thousands of endogamous hereditary groups called Jatis.

The Jatis were grouped formally by the Brahminical texts under the four well known categories (the varnas) viz Brahmins (scholars, teachers, fire priests), Kshatriyas (kings, warriors, law enforcers, administrators), Vaishyas (agriculturists, cattle raisers, traders, bankers), Shudras (artisans, craftsmen, service providers). Certain people like foreigners, nomads, forest tribes and the chandalas (who dealt with disposal of the dead) were excluded altogether and treated as untouchables. Although generally identified with Hinduism, the caste system was also observed among the ancient Persians and followers of other religions in the Indian subcontinent, including some groups of Muslims and Christians, most likely through cultural assimilation over centuries." **(Caste system in India – Wikipedia)**

We see signs of cultural hindrances to compassion in Job's three friends. Stephen M. Miller says concerning Job's three friends lack of compassion,

> *"They say God is punishing him* **(Job)**. *That's a common belief in ancient times. Blessed people are blessed because God is rewarding them for living a good life, and afflicted people suffer because God is punishing them for sin. Many Bible experts say that the whole point of Job's story is to refute this warped theology. Jesus later refuted it too."* **(Stephen M. Miller – The Complete Guide To The Bible, page 151)**

Again, we see the story of the blind man and the disciples foolishly arguing who brought the curse; him or his parents. Even in Judaism there are cultural hindrances to compassion. That is one of the reasons why Christ's ministry was so radical.

Duplicity and Bad Doctrine

This reminds me of a movie I should never have watched. There are several movies I should have avoided in my lifetime, but one stands out here: Legion. If you don't know what the movie, Legion, is about or you are pretending you don't know what I am talking about, this movie is about the angel Michael. The movie begins with Michael arriving on earth with his wings removed. He came to earth on a mission. This mission was not from God. In fact, his mission was against God. In this movie God was pretty fickle. God lost patience with humanity and decided that He was done with them. He wanted to wipe them out. He set in motion a plan. In this plan, angels would go possess the weak minded and use them to bring death and destruction to the earth. So, these angel possessed people began manifesting and killing people.

Michael, unlike God, still had faith that humanity could get past their wickedness. He knew of a child that would be born that would be the second Messiah, which would save humanity. . . again. God had sent this child into the world, but then changed His mind and wanted the child destroyed.

There is a dialogue between the angel Michael and the angel Gabriel. Gabriel, God's Yes Man, wanted to give God what He wanted which was death and destruction, while Michael, the Naughty Angel, wanted to give God what He needed, which was the salvation of man. In the end, Michael convinced God to spare the Messiah child and hold back His anger. The End.

The whole story sounds ridiculous, but it matches the doctrine of a majority of the church today. Let's look at this with the Earthquake in Haiti thrown into the sequel for this movie which has not been made yet.

Legion Part 2

(You have to read this with that low, exciting movie narrator voice.) God changed His mind again, again, again. His anger was aroused once more and He lost His cool. He decided that He was done with the people of Haiti for their witchcraft. He was going to destroy them. He told the Angels, Michael and Gabriel, of His plan to totally destroy the Haitians. Phase One of the plan was to send angels into the tectonic plates and cause an earthquake that would bring desolation, destruction and death. They did just that. They caused a devastating earthquake.

God's plan was set in motion, but Michael still had faith in the Haitians. He believed that they could change and be made right again. He travelled to the earth and began rallying up the church to send relief and help to the Haitians. Gabriel knew that Michael was going to do this so he began rallying up the church as well. He got the majority of the church to say that God wanted to destroy the Haitians. They began preaching that it was God's judgment. Gabriel got the church to give God what He wanted, while Michael got the church to give God what He needed. In the end, God changed His mind again and began blessing the relief work of the missionaries there. (End movie narrator voice)

This story sounds crazy, but this is the kind of junk that is going on right now in the church. I had a teacher at Bible College who preached that junk. Not with those words exactly, but his doctrine matched up with it. In other words, God is always getting angry and raining down judgment and wrath. When He is done with His temper tantrum, we as the church are to go and use the Great Commission to clean up His mess.

Wow. What a message! No wonder so many unsaved people say things like, "I won't become a Christian because the Bible is full of contradictions." What they are really saying is that the message that was preached to them was full of contradictions.

We need to not be a hindrance to the goodness of God in the earth with our cultural, traditional and religious road blocks.

Now we are ready to dive into the crazy mess that happens after Job's three friends arrive.

Larry, Moe and Curly

With friends like these, who needs enemies? I guess you could call them frienemies.

> **Job 2:11 (HCSB)** *"Now when Job's three friends – Eliphaz the Temanite, Bildad the Shuhite, and Zophar the Naamathite – heard about all this adversity that had happened to him, each of them came from his home. They met together to go and offer sympathy and comfort to him.*
>
> *When they looked from a distance, they could barely recognize him. They wept aloud, and each man tore his robe and threw dust into the air and on his head. Then they sat on the ground with him seven days and nights, but no one spoke a word to him because they saw that his suffering was very intense."*

The ancient eastern cultures are so different from ours. Mourning and wailing seemed to be a bit of a sport in those cultures. Mourning was a cultural art. There are two Middle Eastern cultural practices involving grief that come to mind here. Both of them are still in practice today in parts of the Middle East. The first one is what we just read in the above passage; weeping aloud while ripping your clothes and throwing dust and ashes in the air and on your head. Wayne Blank says concerning the wailing custom of wearing sackcloth and ashes:

> *"Although the modern-day idea of "wearing sackcloth" is often that of someone dressed in a burlap grain bag and arm holes cut in it, during Bible History its appearance was quite different.*

Sackcloth was most often made of coarse, black goat's hair. As its name indicates, it was used for sacks, but was also customarily worn by mourners (in some countries, the ancient custom is still faintly seen today when mourners wear black arm bands at funerals), or as a sign of deep repentance and humility. Ashes were often included as a further symbol of personal abhorrence and chagrin."

(Sackcloth and Ashes – Wayne Blank)

The second custom is known as Professional Mourning. Simon Nguyen says it best:

"In many Asian countries, it is quite common and popular for the family of the dead person to hire professionals to take care of the weeping and crying parts essential to any funeral. There are two levels of 'pay to cry' service. The basic service includes weeping and crying. The premium service includes dramatic sobbing and beating of one's chest.

Professional mourners are expected to follow standard protocols; their services are retained through the entire length of the funeral. In order to be a professional mourner, one has to spend many years as an apprentice; some even have to pass professional examination.

Clients won't accept anything less than a seasoned professional. This is due to the fact that in many cultures, weddings and funerals are considered to be the two most important moments in one's life. . . For many people, funerals are serious business. Assigning a rookie to perform a funeral's most sacred function is considered an insult."

(Bizarre: Professional Mourners - Pay to Cry - Simon Nguyen, Yahoo! Contributor Network)

We just recently witnessed this very practice with the passing of Kim Jong Il of North Korea. For many days the people wailed and moaned while beating their fists on the ground. It was the perfect example of the art of mourning.

While, in Job's day, it may have been the adequate cultural response, it was not the adequate biblical response. Here we see the cultural hindrance starting to elbow rudely into the midst. I'm wondering if, in their culture, this kind of behavior was what was known AS sympathy and comfort.

Seven Days of WHAT?!

We have two possibilities here created by their cultural hindrances. One, they either did their wailing as a show of support and comfort for Job and then afterward remained absolutely silent for seven days straight, or two, they continued wailing and ripping their robes and beating their chests and throwing dust and ash in the air and on their heads for seven days straight. I think that either one is equally bad, and yet, either one would have been the accepted cultural response in their day.

If they sat silently for seven days, they may have been moved to compassion because they would have been forced to look upon their friend in his condition for an entire week. This is one of the ways that culture and blind piety can destroy a society.

If they wailed and threw themselves around for seven days straight they would not have been able to focus on the more important matter of what to do with their friend who desperately needed their help. They would have been doing their religious and cultural duty by making a public show with their wailing, and in that society, nothing more may have been needed.

For seven days they didn't talk to Job, but they sat idly by as their friend was wasting away with an incurable disease. SEVEN DAYS! If they were wailing the whole time, did they stop to eat? Did they go to sleep? If they did go to sleep, did they wake up and commence with wailing again? Did they take turns or go in eight hour shifts? Did they copy Job's wailing? Did they have to put on new sack cloth robes to rip when they destroyed the old ones? You can only rip a piece of material so many ways until it can no longer be classified as clothing and stay on your body. Seven days is a long time to be ripping your clothes off constantly. That is a lot of clothing to destroy. Did they bring seven days worth of wailing wardrobe? Were they in competition for who was the best wailer? You can only do so much before your body gives out from the forced emotional drama.

It is a wonder that they were able to talk after all of this. It would have been quite the spectacle! You can be sure there was a crowd of people that gathered for the sheer entertainment of it. It was an ancient reality show! Maybe there were some people capitalizing on it. "Hot dogs! Get your hot dogs, here!"

On the other hand, if they were silent, how awkward that silence must have been for Job! How do you think you would have handled it if you were helplessly dying from an incurable disease, lying in a pile of rubble and ashes where your house used to stand and your friends were just sitting there watching you die for an entire week without offering any comfort, food, medical help or shelter? They never offered to bind up his wounds. They never brought him a bowl of soup. They never offered to get him and his wife a place to sleep. They never even spoke to him! SEVEN DAYS! They showed no compassion at ALL. No wonder Job erupted with his rant of wanting to die! I would too if I had to go through what he went through and then had to deal with these three good-for-nothings! Let's look at what he said again:

> **Job 3:1-6 (HCSB)** *"After this (seven days of ridiculous drama) Job began to speak and cursed the day he was born. He said, 'May the day I was born perish, and the night when they said 'A boy is conceived.' If only that day had turned to darkness! May God above not care about it, or light shine on it. May darkness and gloom reclaim it, and a cloud settle over it. May an eclipse of the sun terrify it. If*

only darkness had taken that night away! May it not appear among the days of the year or to be listed in the calendar.'"

I think that Job was teetering on the edge and may have stepped back with some coaxing and encouragement, but after the seven day stunt they pulled, Job gave it a running and flying leap. I believe they were Satan's "Plan C". Plan A of destroying everything didn't work. He still blessed God. Plan B of afflicting him with incurable sores didn't work. He still blessed God. Plan C of Satan using his friends to push him over the edge worked perfectly. It usually does. Stephen M. Miller says concerning Job's friends:

"Sadly, when they do start talking their words are harsh enough to qualify as bonus torment – as though the Accuser got God's permission to send them. These three men take Job's misery into a new dimension – from physical to spiritual. Job has already lost just about everything this world has to offer: riches, family, health. That couldn't be much clearer, with Job sitting on a pile of ashes and scratching around his pus pockets. Now his friends arrive and call him a sinner."

(Stephen M. Miller – The Complete Guide to the Bible – page 150-151)

So, after they create seven days of absolute misery for their friend, they turn to Job and say, "SINNER," adding insult to injury.

What's In A Name?

Before we go further, I want to talk about their names. In Biblical Stories, names are everything. Let's look at Eliphaz. Eliphaz literally means "god of gold". Eliphaz was a graven image or idol shaped out of gold.

Bildad had an even worse name. Bildad means "Baal has loved". Baal was the one false god that the Israelites strayed from God to worship the most. Every time they fell into worshiping false gods, Baal was right there in the midst of it with all of his perversions.

You think Bildad was bad? How about Zophar? Zophar was an access point for the demonic. Just like the pyramids were access points for the Egyptian gods and goddesses, Zophar was a high place. It was an open door for the demonic to enter through.

So there you have it. Job's three friends' names were all steeped in idolatry. We will go into idolatry more in a later chapter.

What is interesting is that Job's friends seem to start out right with what they say, but then, as you read further, it starts to head down a wrong path. It's like when a Jehovah's Witness comes to your door and you invite him in. At first, what he says sounds good, but as you get deeper into what they teach, you see the error begin to surface.

At first, Eliphaz begins by praising Job for the blameless and upright things that he has done. He seems very kind with his words. And then, all of the sudden, he starts veering off into grave accusations. For the sake of your sanity and keeping your attention, I will refrain from delving deeply into the conversation of those who are in love with the sound of their own voices. That's what it boils down to. I have pulled one pivotal part of each argument from these three colloquial friends to share which will give you an idea of how much of a friend to Job they are not. Like I said, let's start with Eliphaz.

5:17 *"See how happy the man is God corrects;*
so do not reject the discipline of the Almighty. For
He crushes but also binds up. He strikes, but His
hands also heal."

Here he is saying that God has struck Job and that Job should be happy that God corrected him! "Gee, thanks, God, for killing my children, destroying everything I own and afflicting me with incurable sores! I am so happy now!" Not only that, but he is calling it correction and discipline which says that Eliphaz is accusing Job of bringing this calamity by sinning!

What have we learned about God's role in this? God was not the author of this calamity. It had nothing to do with discipline or correction. It was all about Job and his fear tying the hands of God and enabling Satan to wreak havoc.

The next twenty five chapters are filled with Job's "friends" trying to label him as a wicked man and that Job had brought it upon himself. (Well, he did bring it upon himself, but not with wickedness.) All the while, Job is in excruciating pain, completely exhausted physically, mentally and emotionally, suffering from hunger and has no place to rest.

Let's look at what Bildad had to say;

> **Job 8:3 *"Does God pervert justice? Does the Almighty pervert what is right? Since your children sinned against Him, He gave them over to their rebellion. . ."***

Here his second friend is starting to go in for the kill and blame the calamity on Job's children and their rebelliousness. Is that the kind of thing you say to a friend who has just lost all of his children? Such loving friends! If I were Job, Bildad would have been swallowing his teeth after that remark. I'm sure that if Job had not been so sickly and had more strength, Bildad might have had some argument on that one.

The conversation between God and Satan had nothing to do with Job's children. Satan never brought their wickedness up in his conversation with God. This calamity was all about Satan trying to destroy Job. His children were just the icing on Satan's cake. I've actually heard "Hellfire and Brimstone" believers say this kind of terrible thing to a grieving parent concerning the passing of one of their children. Things like, "You did everything you could, if only they had listened, the Lord would have spared them." It's that same wretched condemning religious spirit that had manifested in Job's three friends.

I could write a whole other book just on how not to deal with grieving parents by using the examples of Job's three friends. If you ever want to know what kind of attitude you SHOULDN'T have as a believer, Job's three friends are the best examples to glean, or should I say NOT glean from. I will say it again. STOP QUOTING FROM THESE MEN! Unless, of course, you are pointing out their obvious flaws.

Let's move on from this atrocity to an even greater one with Job's friend, Zophar.

> **11:4-5 *"You have said, 'My teaching is sound, and I am pure in Your sight.' But if only God would speak and declare His case against you, He would show you the secrets of wisdom, for true wisdom has two sides. Know then that God has chosen to overlook some of your sin."***

> **11:11 *"Surely He knows which people are worthless. If He sees iniquity, will he not take note of it? But a stupid man will gain understanding as soon as a wild donkey is born a man!"***

Wow. Zophar is truly heartless.

I don't know where Job got his friends from, but I'm sure that after this Job found some new ones. All three friends blast Job over and over again about the wickedness of Job and of his children when they should have been showing him compassion. They declare him guilty in God's court.

So many ministers and churches think that God gave them the gavel to slam down judgment on people, organizations, churches, cities, regions and nations i.e. New Orleans with Hurricane Katrina, Haiti with the earthquake, Japan with the earthquake and tsunami, etc. The gavel has never and will never belong to us. The real authority that Christ has given us is in casting out devils, healing the sick, raising the dead and making disciples. As long as we are busy doing that, we have no time for gavels. Let's get back to the story at hand with Job's three friends.

They are so inflated in their own wisdom and sure of their understanding that they steamroll heartlessly over Job with bitter diatribes and accusations. Again, this sounds like some of the churches I grew up in. It is the same haughty stone cold religious spirit found in much of the Hell Fire and Brimstone crowd. Their doctrine is so flawed that it blocks the flow of God's love to them and they become bitter vipers spewing out doctrines of devils. Whatever love they had previously known of God is buried and lost under the rubble of their bitterness.

The Sponge and The Spout

Speaking of blocking the flow of God's love, We as believers are a lot like dish sponges. Let me tell you a little story. There have been a couple times that I have somehow lost the sponge I used to wash dishes. One time it wound up inside the cabinet under the sink. When I found it, it was all hard and shriveled up. All it took to make it soft and absorbent again was to put it under the water and squeeze it a few times. If I were to put it back under the cabinet, over time it would become hard again.

That is what happens when you have a flawed view of God like this. You may have been a soft and agreeable sponge, but you got out from under the spout where the love came out and you wound up all hard, dry and shriveled up. You are no longer soft and pliable, you are hard and scratchy. You are no longer useful as a sponge, and the only way to change that is to get back under the love spout. The only problem is that you no longer believe in that love spout so you are destined to live a life as a hard, shriveled up, angry, accusing sponge that's not good for anything but being scratchy. Job's three friends are like scratchy sponges.

As you read through what these three friends say (30 chapters) you will notice that much of their doctrine matches a majority of mainline Christianity in our society. Newsflash! It's wrong! God addresses it at the end and tells these three stooges that they gave a wrong account of God. Let that sink in for a minute. This is the one time in the Word of God where God shows up without the use of a prophet and says out of His own mouth, "YOUR DOCTRINE IS

WRONG!" That is pretty powerful, and yet I've heard pastors quote some of what these men say AS doctrine. EGAD! God Himself, not a prophet, spoke with His own mouth that it was wrong!

Let's see what God had to say to them. Mind you, this is after Job has a change of heart and started speaking the truth concerning God in the end.

> **42:7-8** *"After the Lord had finished speaking to Job, he said to Eliphaz, the Temanite: "I am very angry with you and your two friends, for you have not spoken the truth about Me, as My servant Job has. Now take seven bulls and seven rams, go to My servant Job and offer a burnt offering for yourselves. Then my servant Job will pray for you. I will surely accept his prayer and not deal with you as your folly deserves. For you have not spoken the truth about Me as My servant Job has."*

OUCH!

I need to mention one overlooked yet profound fact at this point. There is one person whom the Lord did not rebuke. Can you guess who it is? God rebuked Job, the three friends, and the young kid, but He never rebuked Job's wife. She is the only character that did not get a tongue lashing from God. That speaks 1000 volumes in itself!

Isn't it interesting that the one person who is criminalized the most in the Book of Job by much of the Church is the one person whom God did NOT rebuke? How backwards is that?! Actually, what could God have rebuked concerning her? She said one thing and then remained absolutely silent after that. There is a lesson in that.

A Resurrection Hope

Now that we see God's feelings concerning what they had said to Job, we will make a summarized list of what they said that was so offensive to God, but first I need to mention one last thing in this chapter that I feel is a ray of light in this gloomy story. In the middle of the ranting and mouth foaming from Job's friends, Job goes "New

Testament" on us! Job had a resurrection hope. Quoting Stephen M. Miller again,

> *"Go ahead; try to find any reference in the Old Testament to life after death. They're all over the New Testament, but it seems that most people in Old Testament times had no idea they could rise again and spend forever with God. Most Old Testament characters talking about death had nothing to say about an afterlife, though a few mention a shadowy place of the dead where they expect to live with their ancestors. The godly king Hezekiah had an even bleaker take on the afterlife. In a song of praise to God for healing him, he wrote: "For the dead cannot praise You . . . Those who go down to the grave can no longer hope in Your faithfulness. Only the living can praise you as I do today" (Isaiah 38:18-19) Job is an exception. Speaking from what must feel to him like the brink of death, he sounds like a man with New Testament savvy – living 2,000 years ahead of his time: "But as for me, I know that my Redeemer lives, and He will stand upon the earth at last. And after my body has decayed, yet in my body I will see God! I will see Him for myself. Yes, I will see Him with my own eyes. I am overwhelmed at the thought!" (Job 19:25-27)."*
> **(Stephen M. Miller – The Complete Guide To The Bible)**

One of the signs of legalism in a church is the constant mention of wanting to either die or be raptured and go to heaven. The abundant life is not found in legalism; that is for sure.

What God Is Not

Now, let's go to the list of things that God is not.

This is how I am going to lay it out. Instead of writing out the scriptures, I am going to put the chapter and verses and then a brief summary of what Job's friends said next to it. You can read it on your own if you want. I only put the passages where they addressed God. Here it is for your viewing pleasure!

God is (will). . .

- 4:8 – a destroyer of trouble doers and the unjust

- 4:18 – paranoid and untrusting concerning his servants and angels

- 5:12 – a frustrator of the crafty

- 5:13 – a trapper of the wise

- 5:18 – discipline you by crushing you or striking you down

- 8:4 – a destroyer of rebellious children

- 15:15 – paranoid and untrusting concerning his servants and angels

- 20:23 – rain His burning anger down upon the wicked

- 20:24 – pierce the wicked with arrows

- 20:25 – cover the wicked with terrors

- 20:29 – give an inheritance of destruction to the wicked

At first glance, you may say, "But I was taught some of these things in Sunday School!" So was I! One of the teachers in the Bible School I attended taught EXACTLY this demonic doctrine. God said that the things they said about Him were wrong. Those are the things that were said about Him. No more, no less. I left nothing out and I did not manipulate the facts.

Back to the things that God says He's not; here is a scripture that will put it all in perspective:

Romans 2:4 *"Or do you despise the riches of His kindness, restraint, and patience, not recognizing that God's kindness is intended to lead you to repentance?"*

Again, I must mention the angry preachers who preach relentlessly that God destroys trouble doers and the unjust, disciplines you by crushing you or striking you down, destroys rebellious children, rains His burning anger down upon the wicked and gives an inheritance of destruction to the wicked. They use their angry gospel to dismantle the Gospel of Grace. I have to say that I am not completely innocent here. I used to do it, too. I was its poster child for a while.

They seem to despise the riches of God's kindness, restraint and patience and refuse to recognize that it was God's KINDNESS that was intended to lead you to repentance. There is a perfect example in the Bible of a prophet who had that destructive doctrine. This prophet ran away from the call of God because he wanted God to rain down His wrath, rather than show mercy. That prophet, as you probably guessed, was Jonah. God wanted to be merciful, while Jonah wanted the wicked people of Nineveh to be destroyed. And, let me tell you, the people of Nineveh were a very wicked people. It's just one telling example of the contrast between the bad doctrine that we just recognized, and God's unmerited favor and love.

Back to the angry preachers, many of their disciples under their tutelage become dry crusty sponges that are many times angry, judgmental and condescending, prideful and arrogant, and many times looking for a fight, an argument or a debate, just like Job's friends. That is the fruit of Job's Friend's "Angry Gospel". God calls it FOLLY!

Let's talk about this Angry Gospel more in detail in Chapter 10 and discuss its sinister roots.

Chapter 10: *Let's Talk About Idolatry*

Pharisees Before There Were Pharisees

I've already talked about Job's friends and how their very names are idolatrous. We don't know anything about them personally apart from their names, their opinions on Job's situation and God's opinion of them. Well, maybe that's enough.

Let's talk about how their names and their conversation reveal something of their character. All three friends that speak share certain characteristics. They remind me very much of the Pharisees and Sadducees Jesus deals with in the New Testament. Outwardly, they seem to be Godly or God-Fearing men and yet – not. They did the right thing, showing up and lamenting with Job publically. They were there for all to see, as was culturally expected of them. But when they opened their mouths, we found what really lurked beneath.

All three men insinuate that everything is Job's fault – or his children's fault. Of course, nowhere in the Bible do we read that the sins of the children will be visited on their fathers, in fact Deuteronomy 5:9 (NLT) says,

> *"You must not bow down to them or worship them, for I, the LORD your God, am a jealous God who will not tolerate your affection for any other gods. I lay the sins of the parents upon their children; the entire family is affected—even children in the third and fourth generations of those who reject me,"*

God's pretty clear that He will not tolerate idolatry, blaming the parents even as they pass idol worship down to their children. God holds the parent responsible for teaching their children right from wrong, not the other way around. Since Job was obviously dedicated to ensuring his children served God, I don't see how any of what happened could have been their fault EVEN if it was the punishment of God, which I believe I have shown to be not the case here.

Job's friends also seem to enjoy pointing out in as many words as possible how God would NEVER punish the upright. Can't you just hear that tone of "notice *I'm* not having any problems" as they go on and on. And so, by default, Job must not be as blameless and upright as everyone thought he was. Isn't it interesting that none of them went to Job on the side and asked him if there might be something in his life that might be displeasing God? No, instead they automatically started casting blame. Good thing they weren't there that day with Jesus and the woman caught in adultery[10], huh? I wonder if they would have tried to argue that they were blameless then. Sadly, those with the spirit of Job's friends always seem to be with us – then, in Jesus' day and today.

Unfortunately, self-righteousness itself can become an idol in our lives. We get sucked into the perfectionist trap. It's all about the outside appearance, being perfect, looking perfect, and saying the perfect thing. So many people get lost trying to look and act like a Christian and forget that God tells us in 1 Samuel 16:7(NLT),

> *"But the LORD said to Samuel, "Don't judge*
> *by his appearance or height, for I have rejected him.*
> *The LORD doesn't see things the way you see them.*
> *People judge by outward appearance, but the LORD*
> *looks at the heart."*

Job's friends LOOKED good, they did the right thing and they said what sounded like good Bible doctrine – but inside they were gloating in his obvious failure. They were puffing themselves up with their own self-righteousness and accomplishments by reminding Job how low he'd fallen. If they had truly been operating with the Mind of Christ, they would have known that, *"We are all infected and impure with sin. When we display our righteous deeds, they are nothing but filthy rags...* [11]*"*

God created us to worship. But He also gave us free will, which means we can choose to worship Him or to worship something else. Worship is defined as

"The reverent love and devotion accorded a deity, an idol, or a sacred object. Or, the ceremonies, prayers, or other religious forms by which this love is expressed.[12]"

Worshiping Worship

Unfortunately, many stop worshipping God and start worshipping the act of worship. They become so focused on worshipping so that they are seen to worship that they are no longer focused on the One they're supposed to worship. The act or appearance of worship becomes an idol in their lives. This is actually an epidemic in the Body of Christ today, but we will get into that later on.

An idol is defined as

1. a. An image used as an object of worship. **b.** A false god.

2. One that is adored, often blindly or excessively.

3. Something visible but without substance

(www.thefreedictionary.com)

What is or can be an idol then? Obviously there are idols of the graven image kind as well as living people we "idolize" and try to emulate as much as possible. But the third definition is more subtle than the others – 'something visible but without substance.' Outer appearances, perhaps? Visible actions with nothing in the heart to back them up?

In his review of the book Unceasing Worship: Biblical Perspectives on Worship & the Arts by Harold Best, Vernon Charter of Prairie Bible College writes[13],

"Idolatry, as Best has already pointed out, is the inversion of authentic outpouring, the pouring of

---

[11] Isaiah 64:6 (NLT)

[12] www.thefreedictionary.com

[13] Ethnodoxology.com, Vol. 3, No 2

oneself out towards a false god rather than the true. For the Christian, perhaps the most obvious temptation to idolatry lies in turning the legitimate appreciation and celebration of God's good gifts into a worshiping of the gifts themselves. A more subtle but no less insidious danger lies in what Best describes as "worshiping God idolatrously" (p. 164). In fact, "idolatry is the chief enemy of the most fervently worshiping Christian, even to the extent that some of us may end up worshiping worship" (p. 163). The principles in this chapter are among the most heart-searching passages of the book.

These cautions have great relevance for those of us who cultivate and promote indigenous forms of worship, lest we are tempted to regard "heart music" or culturally informed liturgies themselves as agents of renewal or mediators of authentic worship in the global scene. At the same time we must be cautious of knee-jerk reactions to what may, in fact, be clearly idolatrous. Historically, evangelicals have tended to be iconoclasts, and in the process we are slow to recognize the Lordship of Christ over all things.

The glorious thing about God's grace is that he can take an idol and, without destroying it, turn it into nothing in order that it can be changed into merely something to be offered back to him through Christ. If music is an idol, God can burn it clean and turn it into a faith-driven offering.... In this way the arts, along with beauty, quality, variety, results and even continuity, would become one in a radical newness that is always at the ready when God is enthroned over the gods."

If idolatry in the fallen, unsaved world is shaping a god to worship, what would idolatry be in the Christian world? We as Christians are at an even greater risk of being idol worshipers. In our world, we have the problem of shaping God into the person we are comfortable worshipping. This happens when we are trying to avoid change.

There are those who refuse to change when the Holy Spirit moves on them and they became hard. In order to not be convicted and conflicted in their hearts, they gave God their same hateful, judgmental, angry, merciless, wrathful, abusive, negative and apathetic character qualities. They formed their own image of God to worship and made sure He was WHO they wanted to worship. Once Jesus became like them, in their own minds, they never had to change, grow or develop the Mind of Christ. They could decide which attributes of God to believe in and conform to and leave the rest. This is the most common form of idolatry in the church today.

Two Options

The "Angry Gospel from an Angry God" is birthed out of the Christian's reluctance to be transformed by the renewing of their mind into the Mind of Christ. It comes from not wanting to let go of hate, a judgmental attitude, anger, mercilessness, wrathfulness, abusiveness, negativity and apathy. It is how you can reject the Character of Christ, not allowing it to form in you. It comes from not letting go of your rights. It comes from refusing to be wrong and always insisting that you are right. It comes from not surrendering your heart repeatedly. It has its roots in pride, for it takes humility to admit that God's way is better than your own. And lastly, is birthed out of the conflict in your heart.

You have two options to relieve the conflict when the Spirit moves upon your heart repeatedly to surrender. You can either surrender to the Spirit of God and let Him form You into the image of Christ, or you can repeatedly fight it and form Christ into the image you want Him to have. On one end you have true worship and on the other end you have idolatry. Graven image or Image of Christ. The choice is yours.

Bringing up those angry preachers of my youth again, they were all about dismantling the sacred calf of _____ (insert something ominous, shocking and controversial here), when they are the ones who need their own cows dismantled. It's trying to pluck the speck out of your brother's eye before removing the plank from your own. That is why I called it ironic earlier.

Chapter 11: *Job's Countersuit*

Oh, No He Didn't!

Job, after all of the bantering back and forth between him and his friends, finally turns his direction at God. I'm sure if they hadn't showed up and distracted him by pulverizing him with their words over and over, he may have done this much sooner. He begins to affirm his own righteousness. Actually, one of the greatest fertilizers used to speed the growth of self-righteousness is slander and accusation thrown at you. If you have the seed in you, you will begin to defend yourself which speeds up the process.

Let's stop right here for a second and quote God concerning Job's uprightness.

> **Job 1:8 *"For there is no one like him (Job) on the earth, a blameless and upright man, fearing God and turning away from evil."***

I don't know if you have noticed in this book, but I have not called Job "Righteous". Let's get into that for a minute.

The "Righteousness" of Job

So, how can one be righteous and self-righteous at the same time? It's simple. One cannot. I am sorry if your mind exploded. Here is another challenging the status quo moment. Let's look at what God said about Job to Satan in Job 1:8 again.

> ***"Then the Lord said to Satan, 'Have you considered My servant Job, that there is no one like him on the earth, a blameless and upright man, one who fears God and shuns evil?'"***

The first thing I want to mention here is that God did not say that Job was righteous. He said that he was a blameless and upright man.

The Hebrew word for blameless is "tam" (H8552) which means "perfect, complete, one who lacks nothing in physical strength, beauty, sound, wholesome, an ordinary, quiet sort of person, complete, morally innocent, having integrity, one who is morally and ethically pure".

There is someone else who was "tam" in the Old Testament that will give you an idea of what this word is used for.

> *"And the boys grew: and Esau was a cunning hunter, an man of the field; and Jacob was a plain (H8552) man, dwelling in tents." Genesis 25:27*

Does this mean that Jacob was righteous? No. It means that he was a good little momma's boy who was nice on the eyes. He was good looking and had an innocent appearance about him.

The Hebrew word for upright is "yashar" which means "straight, upright, correct, right, level, right, pleasing, correct, straightforward, just, upright, fitting, proper, uprightness, upright, righteous". While righteous is in the meaning, it is not the normal use of yashar. It is not used for one being righteous in God's sight. That is another word.

The word we are looking for here is "tsedagah" (H6666) which means "justice, righteousness (in government) righteousness (of judge, ruler, king), righteousness (of law), of Davidic king Messiah, righteousness (of God's attribute), righteousness (in a case or cause), truthfulness, righteousness (as ethically right), righteousness (as vindicated), justification, salvation, righteousness of God, righteous acts." God never used this word to describe Job.

Do you see how different these two are? Yashar is not the same as Tsedagah. Not even close. It is not the same righteousness that was attributed to Abraham because of his faith. NOT THE SAME. Let's look at that in Genesis 15:6:

> *"And he believed in the LORD; and He counted it to him for righteousness (H6666)."*

NOT THE SAME.

That kind of righteousness is mentioned in the Book of Job many times, but it is not by God. Who mentions it, then? Job calls himself righteous (Tsedaqah H6666) three times. Job says it. Not God.

> *Job 6:29 "Return, I pray you, let it not be iniquity; yea, return again, my righteousness is in it."*

> *Job 27:6 "My righteousness I hold fast, and will not let it go: my heart shall not reproach me so long as I live."*

> *Job 29:14 "I put on righteousness, and it clothed me: my judgment was as a robe and a diadem."*

Isn't that interesting? God didn't ascribe it to him, yet he thinks he owns it? Not only that, but he thinks that his righteousness is greater than God's righteousness. That is just disgusting.

So, we can safely and confidently say that Job was NOT a righteous man in God's eyes. WHAT?! Yes. I just said it. Let that sink in for a minute. Job was a morally upright man who dealt fairly with all man, but he was not righteous in the eyes of God.

Here is the difference between a righteous man and a self-righteous man.

> *"We have sinned, and have committed iniquity, and have done wickedly, and have rebelled, even by departing from Thy precepts and from Thy judgments:" Daniel 9:5*

> *"O LORD, though our iniquities testify against us, do thou it for Thy Name's sake: for our backslidings are many; we have sinned against Thee." Jeremiah 14:7*

These two men are prophets of Israel. They are God's spokesmen. They are considered by all of Israel to be holy, blameless and upright men; yet, in their prayers they take responsibility and ownership of theirs and their people's actions.

123

Do we see that happening ANYWHERE with Job? Nope. The Apostle John says it very plainly:

"If we say that we have not sinned, we make Him a liar, and His Word is not in us." 1John 1:10

Righteous men take responsibility for their wrongdoing. Self-righteous men think that they can do no wrong and blame shift.

WHAT A TWIST!

When that sinks in, think about the fact that God protected a self-righteous, bitter, fearful, legalistic man for a long time and let him prosper, until Satan challenged it. Does that blow your mind?

God didn't have to do anything. There was no covenant here. Job was not justified and righteous in God's sight. He was not a man of faith. And as we learned in a previous chapter, he was absolutely clueless on God's character and ways. He didn't know Him. Yet, God had nothing but good things to say about him. God was protecting him. God was prospering him. God was defending him to Satan. WHAT?!

Now that we have that established, let's look at God's discourse with Satan. Satan is damned for eternity. He is the most wicked, evil, sinister being in the Universe. Yet, when he went freely into the Throne Room of God Himself, he obtained an audience with God who did not kick him out. Satan was allowed to speak his mind and God listened. Not only did God listen, but God granted Satan what he wanted.

If that is the case, that the most evil being in the entire Universe can get an audience with God Almighty, how much more are we given place as sons and daughters of God Almighty? It gives new meaning to "Come boldly to the Throne of Grace". Doesn't it? We always have an audience with God. Always. He is always listening to us 100 percent of the time and we are completely welcome in His presence ALL THE TIME. So much so that He makes His home in US who are His temple, His residence.

See how Good your God is?

Back to Job's "righteousness" or self righteousness, Satan never mentioned self-righteousness in either conversation with God. Some would say that self-righteousness was a last minute development in Job's life when his friends mercilessly and endlessly attacked him with accusations. I don't think it was a last minute development. I think it was there the whole time. It was hidden, almost undetectable. You couldn't tell on the surface that it was there. Remember that Job was good at wearing masks. The masks didn't come off until Job had nothing left to lose. Real squeezing was required before that deeply rooted, almost completely hidden, character trait was able to mature and manifest.

Now we are ready to go into Job's tongue wagging and finger pointing. This is where it gets really stupid. Job states all of the good things that he has done and all of the bad things he has not done. Let's look at that for a minute.

Job's Personal List of Accolades

Here is a list of the "righteous accolades" of Job. I will give chapter and verse along with a brief summary of what he said.

- 30:25 - wept for the less fortunate and needy (Maybe he was also a professional wailer.)

- 31:1 - made a covenant with his eyes and will not look at a young woman (Sounds Islamic to me)

- 31:5 - has not walked in falsehood or deceit (apart from wearing masks and all)

- 31:7 - his steps have not turned from the way, his heart has not followed his eyes; impurity has not stained his hands (From what way is he talking about here? We have established that he was completely clueless about God and His ways.)

- 31:9 - his heart has not been seduced by his neighbor's wife, has not lurked at his door (Taking jabs at his neighbor's loose wife, apparently.)

- 31:10 - has not let his wife grind grain for another man (what does that even mean???) or let men sleep with her

- 31:13 - has dealt fairly with his servants and has addressed every complaint (He's a great manager.)

- 31:16 - has not refused the wishes of the poor, or rejected the widow (Good political move)

- 31:17 - has helped the fatherless, even while Job himself is in an impoverished state (Still trying to keep an appearance. . .)

- 31:18 - has been a father to the fatherless even in his youth and has blessed the widow since he was young (See above comment)

- 31:19 - has clothed the poor and the needy (See above the above comment)

- 31:20 - never cast his vote against a fatherless child (and kissed lots of babies, too!)

- 31:21 - never placed his confidence or trust in gold (*rolls eyes*)

- 31:22 - never rejoiced in his great wealth or in his own acquiring of it (*cough* liar)

- 31:26 - never worshiped the sun, moon and stars (Wow, he gets a gold star sticker! No! Wait! It's a star! Never mind.)

- 31:29 - never rejoiced over his enemy's distress

- 31:30 - never asked for his enemy's life with a curse (and he's never roller skated backwards in an elephant herd, and he's never painted himself blue, put hinges on himself and flung himself in the ocean. . . How many other random things can we fit here?)

- 31:32 - always opened his door to the traveler and the stranger (very courteous. In our culture, we do that for women.)

- 31:33-34 - never covered his transgressions by hiding guilt in his heart because of the fear of the crowds (WHAT?! That is EXACTLY what he is doing now! WOW!)

That's quite the list! One thing was a cultural hindrance. Four may have actually good charitable things if they weren't political moves. Yet, thirteen out of the nineteen things he listed are all things he DIDN'T do. That is another sign of legalism.

One big problem with this list is that Job was building his case against God. And claiming a list like this is affirming your own righteousness. He was, in a way, declaring himself more righteous than God. We all have done this and will probably do this intermittently throughout our lives. That is precisely what Self-Righteousness does.

When you are self-righteous you are saying that your righteousness is good enough or better than God's righteousness and you don't need His. It predates all the way back to Adam and Eve. You can equate The Tree of the Knowledge of Good and Evil to the Tree of Self-Righteousness. Satan tempted them with Godliness apart from God. But you can't have Godliness apart from God. That's an oxymoron. It cancels itself out. Self-Righteousness is the same way.

Let's take a look at another character that shows up in this story; Elihu, the son of Barachel from the Ram Family. He's a young kid with a sharp tongue and an ego problem. What else is new?

Chapter 12: *The Young Maverick*

Look At Me! LOOK AT ME!

Before we go into Chapter 32 where we meet Elihu, the son of Barachel the Buzite from the House of Ram, let's look at his name. This one is kind of funny.

The first part is Elihu. Elihu is broken into two words. The first word is "el". There are a series of words that are connected with this: god, great, idol, might, power and strong. Many have translated it to be god or God. The second word is "hoo". The words connected with this are he, she, himself, herself and self. The most popular and accepted translation of Elihu's name is "God of him". But, you should know by the 13th chapter that I like to challenge the status quo. Elihu can also be translated as "god of self" or "idol of self". Once we get into the rest of this chapter, you will see exactly what I mean.

The second part of his name is Barachel which is also broken into two parts. The first word is "barak". The words connected to this are to kneel, to bless, to congratulate, to praise, to salute and to thank. The second word is "el" which we have learned is god, God, great, idol, might, power and strong. The most popular and accepted translation of Barachel is "God has blessed". It can also be God has praised, God has saluted, God has thanked, God has congratulated, etc. Do you see where this is going yet?

But wait! Notice that his title is much longer and lofty than the elders that spoke before him. Like I said before, names in the Bible give you an idea of what the person is as well as who.

The third part of his name is Buzite. This one has to be tracked back a little. The word here is "Buz". It is from a primitive root; to disrespect, utterly condemn, utterly despise. Well, we are certainly spiraling downward here.

The fourth part of his name is Ram. It means exalt (self), haughty, be lofty, mount up, proud, set up, and breed worms? Breed worms? Wow. This brings it full circle!

Let's combine it all! Are you ready for this? His name means:

"God of Self, whom God has congratulated, the Disrespectful from the House of Pride and Exalted Self who breeds worms." I added that last part for fun.

That is pretty scary! You will see just how fitting his name really is later in this chapter.

Fashionably Late

Now, on to Elihu, Son of Inflated Ego. He arrives on the scene, burning with righteous indignation, stepping off of his four humped organically fed Mercedes Camel that momma bought, in his designer hipster skinny robe and handmade turban made from the fur of organically fed free range mountain goats with a pair of non-prescription thick square black framed glasses made from recycled plastic just for looks, while holding in his right hand his newly acquired Harvard Law Degree for aesthetic purposes, and in his left hand a lactose free, gluten free, caffeine free, taste free organic Soy Chai Latte. Before walking up to these four men he takes an epic selfie for his popular instagram page on his iPhone with the others in the background.

> **32:1-5 "So these three men quit answering Job, because he was righteous in his own eyes. Then Elihu son of Barachel the Buzite from the family of Ram became angry. He was angry at Job because he had justified himself rather than God. He was also angry at Job's three friends because they had**

failed to refute him, and yet had condemned him.
Now Elihu had waited to speak to Job because they
were all older than he. But when he saw that the
three men could not answer Job, he became angry."

What really gets me agitated was that this could have gone a whole different direction, but Elihu chose the same path as the three idol worshiping fools. Not that I'm caught off guard or surprised since his idol is himself. You really can't expect Godliness or compassion from someone who worships himself. If Elihu is not a picture of American Culture in the 21st Century, then I don't know what is.

Just like the others, he chose the cultural response and totally blew it. This was an opportunity for Elihu to show compassion to Job. It would have been great if Elihu had gotten angry for the right reason.

It would have been so much better if Elihu became angry because no one offered Job any compassion. He could have come in and saved the day. He could have scooped Job up and took him to his house to clean and bandage his wounds and prepare for Job and his wife a decent meal and a place to sleep. He could have gathered his friends together to rebuild Job's house. He could have gotten the community to come together and gather their resources and try to restore at least a small portion of what Job lost. He could have even offered Job a listening ear without trying to retort back with correction. None of that happened. I doubt that it even entered into his mind. He was so full of himself that it could not have entered into his mind.

Secondly, in his series of perfectly and eloquently worded speeches that he presents, he only gets a little of it right. He never actually addressed the real issue. What is the real issue? The real issue was never about God prosecuting Job. It was never about Job doing anything unrighteous. It had nothing to do with discipline. It had nothing to do with secret sins.

The real issue was that Job had the wrong perception of God which gave way to fear, bitterness and a nasty case of self-righteousness. Because of these three things the enemy was given license to come in and devastate everything. Not that we should be surprised by this, but not one of these five men came anywhere close to the real issue. Why is that? Every single one of them were self-righteous and bitter. It was a long and uncomfortable parade of wagging tongues.

The only one that had any sort of inkling of what was going on was Job's wife and she shut her mouth after Job compared her, his grieving destitute wife, to a foolish child. Who knows how the story would have gone if she had been given more room to speak. She may have had the keys of wisdom in this whole mess. On that note, let's look at a few things that young Elihu, the Son of Poopeth That Don't Stinketh, had to say when he addressed the three accusers.

> **32:11-13 *"Look, I waited for your conclusions; I listened to your insights as you sought for words. I paid close attention to you. Yet no one proved Job wrong; not one of you refuted his arguments. So do not claim, "We have found wisdom; let God deal with him, not man."***

And so we continue with another round of Job bashing. Yawn. During Elihu's monolog, Job never uttered a word. Maybe he took a nap. I doubt it. It's like being forced to watch an all-day marathon of Keeping Up With The Kardashians. Well, no, I think Job's torment was just a little bit worse.

Seriously, these people have issues. Let's get back to those issues. I am picking out the best parts just for you!

> **32:17 *"I too will answer, yes, I will tell what I know. For I am full of words!"***

You know, that's the problem with us sometimes. We are full of words when we should be full of compassion. This brings up the story of the blind man and the disciples discussing generational curses when they should have had compassion and healed the man. It's the same trap; the same lie; the same vain and foolish arguing. When there is no compassion, there are plenty of words.

132

32:21 *"I will be partial to no one, and I will not give anyone an undeserved title. For I do not know how to give such titles; otherwise, my Maker would remove me in an instant."*

So, Elihu, The Son Of Lofty Titles doesn't want to address others with lofty titles. Excuse me while I roll my eyes and let out a sigh of disgust. He pipes in again after he sips on his lactose free, gluten free, caffeine free, taste free organic Soy Chai Latte while taking another quick epic selfie:

33:2-3 *"I am going to open my mouth; my tongue will form words on my palate."*

Either Elihu is one of those "explain it until it is unrecognizable" kinds of people or he is being disrespectful to these older men. I would say it is the latter since that is part of his lofty title. He's almost done with his inflated ranting and is about to actually offer up some wisdom. . . for a short time of course.

33:8-14 *"Surely you have spoken in my hearing, and I have heard these very words: 'I am pure, without transgression; I am clean and have no guilt. But He finds reasons to oppose me; He regards me as his enemy. He puts my feet in the stocks; He stands watch over all my paths.' But I tell you that you are wrong in this matter, since God is greater than man. Why do you take Him to court for not answering anything a person asks? For God speaks time and again, but a person may not notice it."*

He is defending God here. Job has declared that he is more righteous than God, and Elihu is correcting him for it. Elihu is defending God. That's one of the very few things he managed to get right. Unfortunately, he veers off course again with this:

33:19-22 *"A person may be disciplined on his bed with pain and constant distress in his bones, so that he detests bread, and his soul despises his* *favorite food. His flesh wastes away to nothing, and his unseen bones stick out. He draws near the Pit, and his life to the executioners."*

Again we see Job's suffering being called the discipline of the Lord. It is amazing how each of these men are so convinced that they have God all figured out. Elihu, the Pantene Pro-V Hair Model, is so sure of himself here. He's a typical youth; so much charisma and passion, yet so little wisdom. I doubt that Elihu has been thrown to the wolves of adulthood and experienced life yet. The older I get, the more I know that I don't know all there is to know. Elihu appears to not be at that point in his life yet.

33:10-11 *"Therefore listen to me, you men of understanding. It is impossible for God to do wrong, and for the Almighty to act unjustly. For He repays a person according to his deeds."*

Do you sense a hint of sarcasm in the first sentence? Maybe it's just me. These appear to be more uncouth comments to his elders.

It's like he shoots the arrow with almost perfect accuracy and then, at the very last second, the arrow hits the outer ring; every time. Sure, it is impossible for God to do wrong, and for the Almighty to act unjustly. He got that right and then he killed it with accusations against Job, yet again. Oh, for a man of God to speak the truth here and get to the real issue instead of kowtowing to their cultural hindrances! Actually, the only real man of God here is Job.

In chapter 34 in verses 16 through 30, Elihu presents a case on God's Justice and Righteousness, which is actually pretty good. I am going to weave in and out of it to show you that he does get it right on occasion.

"If you have understanding, hear this; listen to what I have to say. Could one who hates justice govern the world? Will you condemn the mighty Righteous One, who says to a king, 'Worthless man!' and to nobles, 'Wicked men!'? God is not partial to princes and does not favor the rich over

the poor, for they are all the work of His hands. . . . For His eyes watch over a man's ways and He observes all his steps. There is no darkness, no deep darkness, where evildoers can hide themselves. God does not need to examine a person further, that one should approach Him in court. He shatters the mighty without investigation and sets others in their place. . . . But when God is silent, who can declare Him guilty? When He hides His face, who can see Him? Yet He watches over both individuals and nations, so that godless men should not rule or ensnare the people."

This is very good. Job had the audacity to declare himself more righteous than God, and Elihu puts him in his place with a fantastically worded counter argument. It was probably eloquently stated. He undoubtedly took dramatic pauses, and flipped his head around which caused his beautiful long dark hair to glean and shine while offering an occasional wink to the young girls who were there because they heard that their favorite youtube celebrity was there.

His argument is good, but it still doesn't get to the truth of the matter, which is this; God had nothing to do with Job's misery.

34:31-37 *"Suppose someone says to God, 'I have endured my punishment; I will no longer act wickedly. Teach me what I cannot see; if I have done wrong, I won't do it again.' Should God repay you on your terms when you have rejected His? You must choose, not I! So declare what you know. Reasonable men will say to me, along with the wise men who hear me, 'Job speaks without knowledge; his words are without insight.' If only Job were tested to the limit, because his answers are like those of wicked men. For he adds rebellion to his sin; he scornfully claps in our presence, while multiplying his words against God."*

This would be such a wonderful argument if Job was a wicked man, but he is not. Remember that God declared Job to be the most blameless man on the face of the earth; TWICE. Elihu says, "If only Job were tested to the limit..." What do you call what Job just went through, a walk in the park? If only Elihu had been tested to the limit! Let's see how he would handle it!

The Glass Globe

When I was younger, a large department store used to sell these clear glass globes that were full of sand. At first glance, you would think that it was just full of sand. Something would happen, though, when you shook the globe. Seashells would begin rising to the surface of the sand. You would have never known they were there until the globe was shaken. The same is true with Job.

Unshaken, Job appeared on the surface to be ok. When he was shaken to the core, all of the junk surfaced in his life. Junk in this case was his wrong beliefs concerning the character and ways of God, crippling fear, bitterness and self-righteousness. Everything became visible to the world. There's nothing like a life shaking experience to remove all of the façades that we use to hide our junk. So, yes, Elihu, Job had been pushed to the limit.

36:4 *"For my arguments are without flaw; one who has perfect knowledge is with you."*

Oh, the pride of youth. Isn't this what every teenager thinks? "Don't trust anyone over 30 years of age!" This reminds me so much of American Culture in the 21st Century. At this, the elders should have sent him home to his parents. I would have stopped listening at this point if I hadn't stopped already. He is inflated with himself and likes the sound of his own voice. The rest is just Elihu flapping his jaws. He says the same thing over and over and over again. I'm sure that Job has had enough and wants to just die by now in peace, but he can't with all the drama.

Used By God?

I do need to make something clear about Elihu, though. While he may have had the wrong idea with trying to prove everyone wrong, he did not engage in name trashing Job like the three idol worshipers did. Even though we see a huge amount of immaturity on Elihu's part, he was trying to do the right thing. Not only that, but I believe that he was sent by God to try to fix this mess and talk some sense into Job. Yes. I did say that.

We will find later that Job, after he gets it right, is told by God to offer prayers and sacrifices for his three friends. Elihu and Job needed no sacrifice here. God did not include either one.

Confused? My point is, you can be on a mission sent by God to do a work and be totally way out of line in the way that you do it. You don't have to be perfect to have a Word or Message from God. You just have to be willing. Elihu was willing. So, don't disqualify yourself because your motives aren't right enough, or you have an unseen struggle, or some other reason. God just wants your willingness to do it.

With all that said, Elihu still did a poor job here by creating an even worse scene and offering no end to the madness.

Where is the resolution in this ridiculous drama that Job is trapped in? What is the point? Is there no one to defend Job? Is there no one to stand up for him? Where is a defender for Job? Where is one who will come to his rescue? Is there someone? Surely, this is not the end! Surely, Job has not met his demise? Is there anyone?

Chapter 13: *The Great Defender*

Being Put In One's Place

38:1 *"Then the Lord answered Job from the whirlwind. He said, 'Who is this who obscures My counsel with ignorant words? Get ready to answer Me like a man; when I question you, you will inform Me.'"*

This may be directed at Job, but it is also a mockery of the three ignorant men who destroyed Job with their words. The four of them obscured God's counsel with ignorant words; all four of them. Who was speaking last when God interrupted? It was the young, jaw flapping know-it-all, Elihu, who was interrupted by God, not Job. Job actually had shut his mouth seven chapters back. It says at the end of chapter 31 *"The words of Job are concluded"* which means that he was done speaking a very long time ago. Not only that, but the last time one of Job's three friends spoke was in Chapter 25. God was putting Elihu in his place. Those sent by God have a greater responsibility and are held accountable for it on a greater scale.

Remember, when God asks a question, it is not because He doesn't know the answer. It is because he is bringing a floodlight into the situation to uncover it and show it for what it is. Elihu was prancing around all full of himself, running his mouth, dishonoring his elders, and God put him in his place by saying to Job, *"Who is this* (Elihu) *who obscures My counsel with ignorant words?"* Oh, snap! We never heard Elihu speak again.

The Paradigm Shift

The next four chapters are God asking Job endless questions about creation. Why four chapters? Because that is what Job needed. In order to recover from this situation, Job needed a paradigm shift.

Three things got Job into this mess. Do you remember what they were? Fear, Bitterness and Self-Righteousness. If it took Job 30 seconds to get the point, it would have been recorded that God said two or three sentences. Instead, it took a very long time for Job to get God's point. Sometimes it takes us a long time to get the point. If we were open to the point that God was making, we probably would have gotten the point much sooner and never got into our mess to begin with.

When it comes to a situation like the one that Job is in, God would rather we stay in our predicament until we have the paradigm shift, than to get us out of the mess without it. The paradigm shift is much more valuable than the deliverance in this case, because the paradigm shift will keep you from getting into the same predicament in the future. Once you have the paradigm shift, the deliverance will follow suite. It's not about believing until you receive. It's not about naming it and claiming it. It's not about decreeing and declaring that you are a king of the King, or mentioning the cattle on the thousand hills, or giving more in the tithing bucket. It's not about putting an eviction notice or an exit date on your problems. It's not about putting the devil under your feet, while waving a white hanky.

We have so many spiritual exercises that are just that, exercising, when the truth isn't manifesting in your heart. And, if you find yourself in a Job predicament, it wasn't your confession or lack of confession that got you there. It was a heart condition. I'm talking about a chronic issue that cripples your faith. Yes, we are to confess decree and declare, but without the shift in our heart, they are just empty words. The Truth Will Make You Free. And who illuminates the truth to our hearts? The Holy Spirit. There is one thing that blocks the paradigm shift that has to be dealt with. We will see that in a minute in God's discourse with Job.

Here's a few of the questions that God asked Job:

> **38:4-11 *"Where were you when I established the earth? Tell Me, if you have understanding. Who fixed its dimensions? Certainly you know!***

Who stretched a measuring line across it? What supports its foundations? Or who laid its cornerstone while the morning stars sang together and all the sons of God shouted for joy? Who enclosed the sea behind doors when it burst from the womb, when I made the clouds its garment and thick darkness its blanket, when I determined its boundaries and put its bars and doors in place when I declared: "You may come this far, but no farther: your proud waves stop here"?

Why in the world is God asking Job questions like these? In order to understand this, we need to back up to when Job was throwing accusations at God. All of them were statements. He declared what he thought were the character and ways of God. He had no question in his mind. The only questions he asked were not really questions, but were used as insults. They were questions of prosecution. He had God all figured out. It was the perfect storm of fear, bitterness and self-righteousness veiled in pride. There was no room for a paradigm shift in Job's mind because his mind was made up. He knew exactly who God was, what His character was like and even His thoughts. That's messed up, but so many people are dealing with the same thing.

I had this problem myself. I just knew that God was out to get me. I had Him all figured out, but wondered why He always felt so distant. Just like Job, I had a dangerous mixture of fear, bitterness, self-righteousness which was cleverly disguised. You know why God felt so distant and untouchable? It is because intimacy cannot be achieved with someone you claim to know everything about already. I will get to that in a minute. Back to God asking Job a barrage of questions.

In order to overcome this obstacle of Job's made up mind, God began barraging Job with questions that began chipping away at Job's surety. God asked Job questions that he had absolutely no clue about. At first, Job did not know what God was doing. But halfway through the questions he starts to figure it out. We don't know if God ever stopped to give Job time to answer. My guess is that He just kept dishing out questions to make a point to Job. God was chipping away at Job's pride and Job knew it.

Read chapters 37 through 41 on your own. All of it is so good, and putting it in this book would be superfluous and counterproductive. I am just going to give you the main points of it that make the argument.

> **40:1-14** *"The Lord answered Job: 'Will the one who contends with the Almighty correct Him? Let him who argues with God give an answer.' Then Job answered the Lord: 'I am so insignificant, How can I answer you? I place my hand over my mouth. I have spoken once, and I will not reply; twice, but now I can add nothing.' Then the Lord answered Job from the whirlwind: 'Get ready to answer Me like a man; When I question you, you will inform Me. Would you really challenge My justice? Would you declare Me guilty to justify yourself? Do you have an arm like God's? Can you thunder with a voice like His?'"*

God asks Job for an answer and Job gets all "woe is me." He says, "I'm a worm. How can I answer You?" At first glance it appears that Job is starting to get a repentant heart. But what is happening here is that Job is trying to pull a fast one on God. I'll show you in a minute.

This is not the answer God was looking for. God didn't want Job to berate himself. Job got enough of that from three idol worshippers and a disrespectful inflated youth. God had a reason for these questions and it wasn't to push Job down further.

Pride and Pride

Actually, Job pulled the old, "Flip the pride coin to the other side" trick. Pride can be compared to a coin. The "heads" side is pride, while the "tails" side is false humility. He went from, "I know it all", to, "I'm a stinkin' worm." It's the other side of pride. Pride is not necessarily you feeling big in yourself. Pride is actually saying, "I know more than God." When you think more highly of yourself then you ought, that's pride. What is also pride is when you think *more lowly* of yourself then you ought.

If God says, "Job is the most upright and blameless man on the planet and none compares to him" and Job says, "I am insignificant. How can I answer You?" Job is not in agreement with God's perception of him, which is pride. Flipping the pride coin is a way to still retain your right to be right - but have the appearance of humility. You can't have your cake and eat it too. I would much rather deal with someone who has obvious pride than deal with someone with false humility. On a side note, using the pride coin is one of the biggest signs that legalism is at work in your life.

Because Job flipped the pride coin, God had to continue with the endless questions, that is, until Job got the hint. Again, how long would God have continued with the questions? He would have continued until Job gave Him the right answer. Job finally got the hint in chapter 42. What is interesting to note is that Job didn't wait for God to ask a third time. He just chimed in with his answer.

> **42:1 *"Then Job replied to the Lord: 'I know that You can do anything and no plan of Yours can be thwarted. You asked, 'Who is this who conceals My counsel with ignorance?' Surely I spoke about things I did not understand, things too wonderful for me to know. You said, 'Listen now, and I will speak. When I question you, you will inform Me.' I had heard rumors about You, but now my eyes have seen You. Therefore I take back my words and repent in dust and ashes."***

This is the answer that God was waiting for! Job finally admitted that he didn't have God all figured out and boxed up neatly like he thought he did. All of the words that Job had spoken in ignorance, he recanted - all the way back to "The Lord gives and the Lord takes away." I want to mention here that the word "wonderful" can also be translated as "hard". *"Surely I spoke about things I did not understand, things too hard for me to know."*

Job let go of his accusations and his fears. Job finally admitted that he didn't know God and that he was clueless about God's character and ways. He let go of the notion that God was going to make his family an oily stain in the road if they weren't constantly made right before Him. He let go of his case against God. He let go of the lie that he had intimate knowledge of God. He only had second-hand knowledge. He said,

> **"I had heard rumors about You, but now my eyes have seen You. Therefore I take back my words and repent in dust and ashes."**

I said it earlier, and I feel it needs mentioning again. A man with knowledge is always at the mercy of a man with experience. When Job saw and heard God, he realized that what he believed about God and what he was now seeing were two completely different things. Isn't it something when we have a Revelation of God that debunks what we had previously thought was truth? That is why intimacy with God is so important. Intimacy with God is not achievable if you think you have it all figured out. It takes humility in admitting that you don't know all there is to know. And when you admit that to God, He rushes in.

Intimacy with God

This brings up the golden calf of Christianity again. Usually, those with the "Angry Gospel" have never had intimacy with God. They are cold and hard. They are calculated and severe. They are like the cold stainless steel table at the morgue; only good for supporting death. They are proud, which keeps them from learning and growing. They remain the same for years, which to them is a badge of piety. With growth, there is always change, but they never grow because they refuse to change. They have made Jesus into the image they want Him to be, so there is no longer a need for change.

144

If they would just go to God and say, "I've been speaking about things that I don't really understand, things to hard for me to really know. I used to think I had you all figured out, but I had only heard rumors about You and had second hand knowledge, and I admit now that I don't know as much as I thought I did. Give me a revelation of You, Lord. Show me something that I don't know about You. I want to know You for You. I want to have the Mind of Christ formed in me." God would respond to that humility and transparency with a whirlwind of intimacy and they would never be the same! Back to the story:

42:7 *"After the Lord had finished speaking to Job, He said to Eliphaz the Temanite: "I am angry with you and your two friends, for you have not spoken the truth about Me, as My servant Job has."*

Wait a minute! Job just recanted on everything that he said concerning God. Why is God saying that Job spoke the truth about Him? Let me address that question with another question. Did God say this before or after Job repented? He said it after Job repented. And what have we learned about God concerning the forgiveness of sin and transgressions? Forgiveness is immediate. God immediately casts our sins into the sea of forgetfulness, whether it be sin or wrong belief.

Job went from being in opposition to God with his accusations to being in right standing with God after he repented of what he said. In other words, God was saying, "You have not spoken the truth about Me, like my servant Job just did." God was very angry with these idol worshippers and their wickedness. They transgressed against his blameless and upright servant, Job, in the most horrible fashion. God was setting the plumb line for all to see. He was distinguishing blameless Job apart from these three unrighteous men.

Notice that God didn't mention Elihu here. I believe there are three reasons why. The first reason being is that he already rebuked him with, "Who is this who obscures My counsel with ignorant words?" The first rebuke was pretty harsh, therefore there was no need for a second one. The second reason was that he was not steeped in idol worship like the other three that were there harassing Job. The third reason is that God hates epic selfies, instagram and youtube. Just kidding.

Again, what is truly amazing here is that Job just finished changing his mind about God, and God wasted ZERO time in restoring Job. The first thing God did was restore Job's credibility by saying that Job had spoken the truth about God. Job had not before, but all it took was a few seconds for Job to recant and God restored Job's credibility. That was fast!

42:8 *"Now take seven bulls and seven rams, go to My servant Job, and offer a burnt offering for yourselves."*

Notice he never asked Job to do this. He only asked the three "friends". Job kept his integrity and didn't sin this whole time, so no sacrifice was needed for Job. That brings up another point. Job said that he repented in dust and ashes. Why would Job repent if he didn't sin? The term repent there has nothing to do with sin, but everything to do with changing your mind. What were the three things that Job struggled with? Fear, Bitterness and Self-Righteousness. Job let go of all three. He took back what he said and then changed his mind about God. That was it.

This brings us back to the sackcloth and ashes thing. It looks like he was just doing the customary thing, but he was already sitting in a pile of dust and ashes that used to be everything he owned. What I think he was saying was, "I take back what I said and change my mind about God in the middle of my hopeless mess."

He didn't wait for things to get better. He didn't say, "I'll change my mind when you restore my life." No, right in the middle of this dismal unfixable disaster, he changed his mind. It wasn't contingent on God doing anything for Job. That is what made it so genuine and so wonderful! It was what appeared to be Job's first step of faith! Job's trust and confidence in God comes BEFORE God helps him. That is true faith.

42:8b *"'Then My servant Job will pray for you. I will surely accept his prayer and not deal with you as your folly deserves. For you have not spoken the truth about Me, as My servant Job has.' Then Eliphaz the Temanite, Bildad the Shuhite, and Zophar the Naamathite went and did as the Lord had told them, and the Lord accepted Job's prayer."*

Every single negative thing, every single character assassination attempt, every single accusation was destroyed in that one moment. God restored Job's reputation in the community by doing this. He also silenced them by pointing out to everyone that may have been watching this fiasco that they were spreading a doctrine of devils. God also restored Jobs spiritual standing with the community by having him pray for them.

42:10 *"After Job had prayed for his friends, the Lord restored his prosperity and doubled his previous possessions. All his brothers, sisters and former acquaintances came to his house and dined with him in the house. They offered him sympathy and comfort concerning all the adversity the Lord had brought on him. Each one gave him a qesitah (money), and a gold earring."*

The Lord not only restored Job's credibility, reputation and spiritual standing in the community, but He also restored Job's wealth and possessions. My guess is that it was restored very quickly because he lost everything so quick. All his family and friends showed up again. Where were they when Job was sitting in a pile of ashes? Laugh and the world laughs with you. Cry and you cry alone. I've learned that lesson more than once.

42:12 *"So the Lord blessed the latter part of Job's life more than the earlier. He owned 14,000 sheep, 6,000 camels, 1,000 yoke of oxen, and 1,000 female donkeys. He also had seven sons and three daughters. He named his first daughter Jemimah,* *his second Keziah, and his third Keren-hapuch. No women as beautiful as Job's daughters could be found in all the land, and their father granted them an inheritance with their brothers. Job lived 140 years after this and saw his children and their children to the fourth generation. Then Job died, old and full of days."*

So, Job's children were adults before Satan struck him. He must have been in his late 30's to early 40's at least when he lost everything. If that were true, then he was around 180 years old when he died. That is a very long time to live. Only a good, loving, compassionate and merciful God would have done that for Job.

What is astounding to me is that Job worked tirelessly to build a reputation, image, influence and seat of power in the community and it was all destroyed by Satan. His works were burned up in the fire. Literally. Then God comes in and gives it all back to him HIS way. All Job had to do was have a paradigm shift and acknowledge it. So, now Job has a reputation, image, influence and seat of power in the community given by GOD. The first part of his life was by works, while the latter part of his life was by Grace. WOW. Now Job is TRULY rendered righteous. Job gets his righteousness when he lets it go. That is truly our own story.

It is truly amazing how the goodness of God has been hidden in plain sight in the book of Job for so long and very few have seen it.

When Ignorance Really Is Bliss

We are almost to the conclusion of this book. Before we get there, though, I we must first address the obnoxious white elephant interpretive dancing in the middle of the room.

Let's read again Job 42:10b where Job's family came to comfort him:

They offered him sympathy and comfort concerning all the adversity the Lord had brought on him.

STOP THE PRESSES! This unravels everything I've tried to establish in this book thus far! Egad, I tell you! EGAD! No. Nothing is unraveling. Let me establish a few things here.

This for the longest time had confounded me because it wasn't God that had brought this calamity upon Job. And yet nowhere does God tell Job that He didn't bring it upon him. God just had Job admit that he didn't know God's ways like he thought he did. So, what is really going on here?

Not once do we see anywhere in Job that any one of Job's friends or his wife mention Satan as being a part of this equation. Why is that? Are you ready for this? You might need to stop a minute and ask God to prepare your heart and mind for this because this is huge.

God is all the time trying to move us out of overwhelming fear and into overcoming faith. With that said, let me lay down a few truths that will help me establish a mountain of truth that will forever change the way you think about God.

- In the Old Testament, Satan is rarely shown as the direct enemy of the Saints.

- In the New Testament, Satan is always shown as the direct enemy of the Saints.

- In the Old Testament, the enemy of the saints was flesh and blood i.e. armies from rival nations.

- In the New Testament the enemy of the saints was Spiritual.

- In the Old Testament, the only thing that ever had influence over the Spiritual Realm was worship and praise. Reference David playing on his harp which caused demons to flee from King Saul.

- In the Old Testament, the saints had almost no authority over Satan and his minions.

- In the New Testament, the saints have ALL authority over Satan and his minions through Jesus Christ.

Do you notice a pattern here? Rarely was there ever a spotlight shown on the demonic realm in the Old Testament. Why is that? It is because they were powerless against it. They had no authority over it. What protected the Israelites from Satan was The Covenant. Job did not (that we could see) have a covenant with God. God had protected Job and prospered him because of his faith for years until Satan challenged God on Job's fear.

With all of that said, if you knew that you had a powerful and merciless enemy that you were powerless to defeat, wouldn't that cause overwhelming fear? And with that said, wouldn't it be God's mercy to conceal to you that you had that kind of enemy coming against you so that you wouldn't live in constant fear? And with that said, wouldn't it be unimaginable compassion, love and selflessness of God to let humanity blame Him for a time for something that had absolutely nothing to do with Him, so that they would never have to live in fear of that unseen enemy? That is why Job said, "I spoke about things too wonderful to know and too hard to understand." Notice that God didn't declare His goodness to Job. Job wasn't ready for that. He only got Job to admit that he didn't have it all figured out and caused Job to retract what he said and thought about God. He was removing the fear. To shed light on the real enemy would have brought more heartache and fear.

God never helped him understand, because understanding what was truly going on would have brought upon Job an even greater fear. Many times when we don't understand something, and after asking God many times to bring clarity and He doesn't, it may be because God is trying to protect us from something we have no control over.

Sometimes it is what we DO know that can hurt us, so God keeps us from information for a time or maybe even for a lifetime. It is the goodness of God at times that keeps us from knowing things. In this case, Ignorance Is Bliss.

I am sure it grieved God when He was blamed for things that were the enemy's fault, but it was a price I believe He chose to pay to keep fear at bay in Job's story, and fear was the main issue in the story of Job. It is what brought this whole mess upon Job. Fear is what gets us into trouble as well.

God's Solution To The Third Power

God spends so much time in His Word telling His saints "Fear Not!"

> *"For God has not given us a spirit of fear, but of power and of love and of a sound mind." (2 Timothy 1:7 NKJV)*

Notice that Paul mentions three things that God gives us: power, love and a sound mind. Why three things? Because God is so adamant about casting out fear that He involves all of Himself in the process. These three things are the three distinct traits or roles of each member of the Godhead. He gives the Power of the Holy Spirit. He gives us the Love of the Father. AND He gives us the Mind of Christ. He gives us the fullness of Himself to overcome fear. And look at what it does! He gives us power to overcome the enemy! He gives us love to overcome our neighbor! AND He gives us the Mind of Christ to overcome ourselves! Wow! Now that is a packaged deal!

> **"And we know that God causes everything to work together for the good of those who love God and are called according to His purpose for them. For God knew His people in advance, and He chose them to become like His Son, so that His Son would be the firstborn among many brothers and sisters. And having chosen them, He called them to come to Him. And having called them, He gave them right standing with Himself. And having given them right standing, He gave them His glory.**
>
> **What shall we say about such wonderful things as these? If God is for us, who can ever be against us? Since He did not spare even His own Son but gave Him up for us all, won't He also give**

us everything else? Who dares accuse us whom God has chosen for His own? No one – for God Himself has given us right standing with Himself. Who then will condemn us? No one – for Christ Jesus died for us and was raised to life for us, and He is sitting in the place of honor at God's right hand, pleading for us.

Can anything ever separate us from Christ's love? Does it mean He no longer loves us if we have trouble or calamity, or are persecuted, or hungry, or destitute, or in danger, or threatened with death? (As the Scriptures say, "For your sake we are killed every day; we are being slaughtered like sheep.) No, despite all these things, overwhelming victory is ours through Christ, who loved us.

And I am convinced that nothing can ever separate us from God's love. Neither death nor life, neither angels nor demons, neither our fears for today nor our worries about tomorrow – not even the powers of hell can separate us from God's love. No power in the sky above or in the earth below – indeed, nothing in all creation will ever be able to separate us from the love of God that is revealed in Christ Jesus our Lord." (Romans 8:29-39 NLT)

Everything is taken care of by our Amazing God and Father in Heaven. He is so interested in our wellbeing that He has covered all the bases for us. We have nothing to fear; nothing to worry about. He is the same yesterday, today and forever. There is no shadow of turning in him. He will always be exactly the same. There is nothing that we can do that can change His feelings and His love for us. We are secure in Him. Because of that, we can rest. We can relax. We can enjoy Him. We don't have to be worried if He has changed His mind about us. Because of Jesus and the work on the cross, God will NEVER change His mind about us. The case is closed.

What Now?

We got through all of that and I can hear what you are thinking.

"What do Job's trials have to do with me?"

"How do I apply this to my own life?"

"How do I get out of my own crisis?"

Those are three excellent questions! Thank you for asking! To answer the first question of "What do Job's trials have to do with me", the answer is a resounding EVERYTHING! Everyone, at least one time in their life, will go through a season of fire where there is much testing. EVERYONE. It is a part of life. It may not be to the caliber of what Job went through, but it will bring you to a place where choices need to be made to survive and thrive. If you do not have a solid foundation of the grace of God and an accurate picture of His character, you will have built your foundation upon the sand instead of the rock. You won't last. This book is meant to help you solidify that foundation and weather the hard storms.

Job is a picture of all of us; a very exaggerated picture of all of us, but a picture of us, none the less. We all struggle at times with faulty or foggy pictures of God's goodness. We know and see only in part, and our fallen flesh likes to fill in the blanks. The more you know of God's goodness and His perfect character, the less blanks your flesh will be able to fill. I hope this book has helped you fill in many of those blanks.

Your second question was "How do I apply this to my own life?" I've heard it said "Where you have an issue with trusting God the most, that is where is grace is allowed to flow the least."

Start confessing His goodness over the areas you are most uncomfortable with. For instance, if you are having issues in your finances, you are not trusting God in that area, so His grace cannot operate. The best way to trust God in that area is to give generously with a cheerful heart. Giving is the greatest show that you are putting your trust in God concerning your finances.

There are many other examples and issues, but that one seems to illustrate what I am saying the best. Also, find verses in the Word that have to do with your weak area and start confessing them, praying them and meditating on them. Get them from your head into your heart. Begin asking God to grant you a paradigm shift in those areas. Talk to people who are strong in those areas. Sometimes one word of wisdom from another believer is all it takes. Be honest about it. Get some counseling from a church leader. Make a decision and then do it. Don't just decide, but also do. I heard the story of two frogs on a log that says this perfectly.

> **Two frogs were sitting on a log when one of them decided to jump off. How many frogs are left on the log? Two. Just because you decide to do something doesn't mean that you actually do it.**

Make a decision and do it.

The third question you asked was, "How do I get out of my own crisis?" This is the best question of all. The answer is a very hard but liberating one. The title of this book is "Grace In the Flames". Notice that it is not "Grace To Get Out Of The Flames".

Now I know what you are thinking. "What are you?! A Reformationist?!" GOD FORBID! If you haven't figured out what I believe by the 14th chapter, then I don't think you will.

I am a strong believer in the miracle working power of the Holy Spirit. I am Baptized in The Holy Spirit. I speak in other tongues. I believe in divine healing. I prophesy. I believe that we are called to cast out demons, heal the sick, raise the dead, and so on. I have seen many amazing things. I speak to storms and command them to leave. Yes. I believe that ALL are meant to be healed. ALL are meant to be free. ALL are meant to be filled with the Holy Ghost and walk in His power. I am a very radical person. There is no Reformationist here.

While I believe that we can change the atmosphere by the power of the Holy Spirit, I do believe there are times that "All things working together for good" means that we go through seasons of fire where the trying of our faith works patience and many other good things. Sometimes it is more important to overcome within the experience first before you actually overcome the experience. I can say to you that I am the poster boy for this very thing.

Write Another Chapter

Let me share what these past three years have been for me. On April the 27th of 2011 I self-published a much shorter version of this book and I called it "A Second Look At The Book Of Job". It was around 95 pages and I had sold 100 copies of it. I was married at the time and we were living in Tennessee where I was leading worship at a church in the mountains. I decided to send a copy of the book to a friend from Bible School who had started his own publishing company. He contacted me and asked that I pull the book out of self-publication because he wanted to give me a contract and publish my book. We had set a release date of October 2012. It would be published the right way with all the bells and whistles that come with a publishing contract. I was well on my way to success. It felt great.

However, things began falling apart in my own life. To make a long story short, I lost the worship leader position at the church, our finances were in shambles, and we had no choice but to move and start over. . . again.

My wife and I decided to move to Fayetteville, North Carolina to be close to family. So, in June of 2012, we packed up and moved in with them in Fayetteville, North Carolina. At this time, the Holy Spirit began telling me that He wanted me to add another chapter to the book and it would be about "Overcoming A Job Experience." (Doh! Insert ominous thematic music here.)

Once we got situated and had been there about a six weeks, I called my publisher. I told him what the Holy Spirit said about writing another chapter. We decided to push back the publication date to an unspecified time so that I could write this chapter.

THE NEXT DAY my wife told me that she wanted a divorce. Within two weeks I was homeless and destitute. I had no job and knew no one. I was on my own with ZERO support and no one to turn to. And I am going to say what you are thinking, You can't write a chapter on Overcoming A Job Experience without overcoming a Job experience. I should have seen that coming. (smacking my forehead) No, I don't believe God thrust me into a Job experience. I believe my bad choices thrust me into it and God was making the best of a bad situation. Remember, all things work together for good to them that love the Lord.

To make a long story short, I went through two years of hell which included some homelessness, shame, humiliation, deep depression, poverty, hopelessness, suicidal thoughts, etc. It was truly what you would call "The Dark Night Of The Soul".

The message of this book is very real to me. I have found God's grace in the flames. I know what it is like when there seems to be no light at the end of the tunnel, and everything I have tried has failed or backfired. I have sat at busy intersections fighting off the thought "If I pull in front of that truck, I can end it all right now." There are a thousand ways to die, but finding God's grace in the flames has made me want to live. It has helped me find purpose.

Just like Job, in the midst of my dark situation, I find myself reaching out to those less fortunate. I have discovered market place ministry, and it is amazing. Actually, they seem to be finding me. I have found that in taking care of them, God takes care of me. I am still here. I am still alive. My faith is strong. I have the peace of God. I have learned to be content whether I abound or am abased. Sure, I still have moments where anxiety sets in, but God is always there. He is keeping me.

Freedom In The Furnace

I have found that the longer I am in the furnace of affliction, the less I smell like smoke. I am also finding that the ropes that had me bound for years are turning into ash and are falling off. I know that my God is faithful. He is able to keep me in any situation, no matter how dark. I have turned my attention from finding the light at the end of the tunnel to being the light in the tunnel.

I am confident in God's Grace. I am secure in His Love. Like a tree planted by the waters, I shall not be moved. I know that every fire is a controlled fire. What was meant for evil from the enemy always turns out for my good because all things work together for good to them that love the Lord and are called according to His purpose.

I don't care what gets in my way, I'm not going anywhere. I will bloom wherever God plants me. I am His workmanship, crafted in His design. I will accomplish that which He has destined for me to do. My future is bright. My course is set. My outcome is determined.

No matter how dark it gets, I will just shine brighter. If whatever dark situation I am in never improves, my heart and mind will continue to improve until it is more painful for the situation to be around me than me in the situation.

No matter what, I am being refined. No matter what, I am growing. No matter what, I am changing. It is all good. I finally understand what Paul was saying in Philippians 4:11b-13:

> **". . . for I have learned how to be content with whatever I have. I know how to live on almost nothing or with everything. I have learned the secret of living in every situation, whether it is with a full stomach or empty, with plenty or little.**

For I can do all things through Christ who gives me strength."

Paul learned to overcome within the crisis. He learned, in a sense, to appreciate the pain. It seemed that the darker his situation became, the brighter he shined. He became free while he was chained to a wall in a bitterly cold, pitch black, rat filled, roach infested germ ridden, horrible smelling prison cell deep within the ground. He was more free in his chains than the prison guard standing watch outside of his cell. That is truly what it means to be an overcomer. That is truly what it means to be more than a conqueror. It's when not even death can snuff you out. The harder it gets, the stronger your message becomes until you yourself become the message.

What is awesome is that, no matter what Paul went through, his belief in the miracle working power of the Holy Spirit did not change. At the end of his life, he still believed in divine healing for all. He still believed in raising people from the dead. He still held fast to his faith. The Gospel of Grace remained The Gospel of Grace. He did not change his beliefs to match his dilemmas.

So, I challenge you today to NOT take a jackhammer to your foundation every time someone doesn't get their healing, or deliverance or breakthrough. We never know the whole story, but what we can be sure of is the Grace and Power of God, and that He never changes. His will is that all be healed.

If you find yourself in the fiery furnace of affliction, be encouraged. Look around and you will see One who looks like the Son of God dancing in the flames near you, and at the end you will dance out of it without the smell of smoke.

We are finally to the "Spiritual and Practical Application" part of the story! I know that you were wondering when this was coming.

Seriously and Obsessively Over and Above

Let's depart from my story and the story of Job for a few minutes to take a much needed, strategically well placed bunny trail with a brief totally unneeded disclaimer.

In case you haven't figured it out by now, I am BIG on God's Grace. There. I said it. I can't undo that, can I? That's ok. I happen to know what God's Grace has done in my life and how it radically changed everything: my identity, my personality, my character, my heart, etc. I don't take the Grace of God lightly.

Yet, Grace is such a taboo word in the Church right now. Many legalistic church leaders have turned it into a four-letter word. They get upset when if someone has the audacity to say that God's Grace is powerful enough to overcome and eradicate sin. What do they call it in the legalistic community when you are big on God's Grace? They call it Hyper Grace.

There are now several books written by legalistic believers where they try to dismantle the Grace Movement by connecting it with the Universalist Movement, which is totally unrelated. Most of the ministers in the Grace Movement preach that you must be born again by confessing with your mouth and believing in your heart that Jesus Christ is the Son of God and that God raised Him from the dead. And these "ministers" would know that – if they were actually paying attention.

In fact, if you feel very comfortable in remaining in your habitual sin, knowing the price that was paid for your redemption and what Christ has done for you, I doubt that you ever really accepted Christ in the first place. His Grace is a Paradigm Shifter and a life changer, and if you are comfortable with sin after the cross, I have a few rather serious questions about your salvation experience.

Back to those authors, it sounds to me like they learned how to share "truth" and connect random dots like some sensationalist journalists have. I detest scandalous exposé Christian Media, by the way. What these authors don't realize is that Paul called Grace "Hyper Abounding Grace".

Romans 5:20 says:

> *"Moreover the law entered, that the offence might abound. But where sin abounded, grace did much more abound:"*

The words "much more abound" are a pretty weak translation of what Paul actually said. The Greek word for "much more abound" is the compound word "hyperperisseuo" or "huperperisseuo". It is two words put into one. Let's look at it here. We have "hyper" and we have "perisseuo".

The modern words "super" and "hyper" comes from the Greek word "hyper" or "huper". What? Oh, no! I am taking a HUGE stretch and assumption there! Wow! Anyway, what does it mean?

It means, in the Greek, "over, beyond, more than".

The modern word "hyper" has many uses. In Dictionary.com it says:

> *"overexcited: over stimulated: keyed up, seriously or obsessively concerned: fanatical: rabid: a prefix appearing in loanwords from Greek, where it meant "over," usually implying excess or exaggeration (hyperbole); on this model used, especially as opposed to hypo', in the formation of compound words (hyperthyroid)."*

I hope that you see it is the exact same word here. I love how Paul put it here. He completely shatters the idea that the law (after the Cross) is greater than God's grace.

Back to the story at hand here, the word is "hyperperisseuo". Perisseuo is translated as:

> *"to exceed a fixed number of measure, to be left over and above a certain number or measure, to be over, to remain, to exist or be at hand in abundance, to be great (abundant), a thing which comes in abundance, or overflows into one, something falls to the lot of one in large measure, to redound unto, turn out abundantly for, to abound, overflow, to be abundantly furnished with, to have in abundance, to be pre-eminent, to excel, to excel more than, exceed, to make to abound, to furnish one richly so that he has abundance, to make abundant or excellent."*

Phew! That is intense! Paul, in this passage, uses two ridiculous words to describe the Grace of God in comparison to the Law of Moses. Let's look at what Paul said again with this understanding:

> *"Moreover the law entered, that the offence might abound. BUT where sin abounded (past tense), GRACE overexcitedly, fanatically, rabidly and in in much excess, abundantly excels more than, exceeds and overflows in much larger measure than the offense of the law."*

Let's continue with what Paul was saying here in Romans 5:21 through 6:1:

> *"That as sin hath reigned unto death, even so might grace reign through righteousness unto eternal life by Jesus Christ our Lord. What shall we say then? Shall we continue in sin, that grace may abound?*

God forbid. How shall we that are dead to sin, live
any longer therein?"

At first glance, you would think that Paul just contradicted himself here. Well, at a legalistic glance, yes. But if you know the power of God's Grace like I do, you would know that Paul is reiterating and fortifying what he just said.

"That as sin hath reigned unto death, even so might
Grace reign through righteousness unto eternal life
by Jesus Christ our Lord."

By the way, "might" doesn't mean "maybe" here. It is the same word that "reign" is. They are both "basileuo" which means:

"to be king, to exercise kingly power, to reign, of the
governor of a province"

What Paul is saying her is:

"Like sin has governed and ruled unto death, even
more so Grace reigns and governs through
righteousness unto eternal life by Jesus Christ our
Lord."

EVEN MORE SO!

Notice that it doesn't say righteousness governs through grace. It says Grace governs through righteousness. Just thought I should throw that in there.

"What shall we say then? Shall we continue in sin,
that grace may abound? God forbid. How shall we
that are dead to sin, live any longer therein?"

If you are legalistic and don't have a full understanding of the Grace of God, you are going to think that this means, "Paul is saying, "NOPE! This does not give you a license to sin! Don't even think about sinning!"

164

That's pretty weak thinking if you ask me. Since when has anyone ever needed a license to sin? Sin happens. Without license. Duh.

What Paul is saying here is this:

"What do we do from here? Continue on in your previous identity with an unregenerate mind in the life of sin you knew without Christ and His redemptive life giving and radically transforming power? That is now impossible because of His Super Abounding Grace. You are DEAD to sin and can no longer live in it. It no longer has power to rule over you. You are no longer under it's jurisdiction and reign. You are now under the reign of Super Abounding, Overcoming, Life Changing Grace."

We are new creatures. We are no longer bound by our old identity. Grace now hyper abounds in our lives. It is no longer about trying to live right. Now we have HIS identity and HE lives through us. It is about living in Jesus and His Grace reigning and governing us through His Righteousness. Once you understand that, you cannot continue on with your previous identity, because you have a NEW mind. You are now dead to sin and cannot live in it. The only way to live in your sin is to have a shallow understanding of God's Grace where you think that God is constantly holding sin to your charge like you are of your old identity.

Insulting God's Spirit and Trampling Jesus

This is also addressed in Hebrews 10:28-29 HSCB:

"If anyone disregards Moses' law, he dies without mercy, based on the testimony of two or three witnesses. 29 How much worse punishment do you

think one will deserve who has trampled on the Son of God, regarded as profane the blood of the covenant by which he was sanctified, and insulted the Spirit of grace?

The gist of the Book of Hebrews is that the Messianic Believers were being led astray by false doctrine. They were being led to believe that they were still bound under the law of Moses and had to keep every law in order to be righteous. They were going back to the types and shadows to make them the reality, which in turn turned the reality of Christ into a type and shadow. They were starting to despise God's Hyper Abounding Grace. They were pushing aside and trampling over their Savior to get back to the Law that couldn't save them.

What the author here is saying is: If you weren't safe before in your transgression under the law, how much more unsafe you are now if you trample over or discount the Son of God, insult His Spirit of Grace and count his blood as less than it is?

Legalistic preachers say that the Grace Movement cheapens Grace. Not true. We see here that LEGALISM cheapens Grace. Not only that, but it tramples over the Son of God on it's way back to the types and shadows of the law, it regards the Blood of Christ as less than it is, and it insults The Spirit of Grace.

What is an insult?

In Dictionary.com is says:

> *"To treat or speak to insolently or with contemptuous rudeness: affront, to affect as an affront; offend or demean, to attack; assault, to behave with insolent triumph; exult contemptuously."*

That is what self-righteous or legalistic people do. They treat or speak with contemptuous rudeness to God's Spirit of Grace. How do you do that? To believe that the Law trumps Grace and that it is now YOUR responsibility to make yourself right with God by YOUR OWN

WORKS (through the Law), what you are doing is saying rather self-righteously that you have greater power than the Spirit of Grace. You are saying that the Blood of Christ wasn't enough. You are saying that Christ's sacrifice didn't do a whole lot. You are saying that what God did is not as great as what YOU can do. You are trampling down the Son of God. You are hurling INSULTS at Him. You speak with contemptuous rudeness towards the Holy Spirit when you say, "Eh. What You did was not enough, so I am going to have to finish what You started. Nice try, though. You get an "A" for effort."

And how do you trample on Christ? One thing that I have found about those who strongly believe in the Grace of God is their REVERENCE for what He did on the Cross. They see Him as one who has triumphed over sin. He is exalted as Lord over All (including sin).

If you don't believe that His Grace is sufficient, you are lowering Him to your own level. You don't have reverence for what He accomplished. In fact, you think that you can do more than Him by justifying yourself through the law. You put Jesus Christ below yourself when it comes you rendering yourself righteous by your deeds and not what He has done. If He is below you, it is very easy for you to trample Him under your feet.

Bottom line, if you think that you can justify yourself through the law, if Jesus's unfinished work plus your unfinished work equals a job well done, if you think that you can overcome sin without His radical Grace, if you think that what Christ accomplished wasn't enough and so you have to add to it, you have just spoken insolently and rudely, in an attacking way towards the Blood of Christ, the Son of God and The Spirit of Grace and you are in worse danger than those who were without Christ.

Ouch.

And concerning the Book of Hebrews, the whole letter is packed with this message. So much so that there is a sect of Messianic Christians (some, not all) who want the Book of Hebrews removed from the Bible because they think it is anti-Semitic. It challenges their works

167

driven mentality and theology. It pulls the "attainting one's own righteousness" rug out from under them, so to speak. That's pretty sad and very dangerous to think that you can earn your righteousness by practicing types and shadows whose sole purpose was to point the way to the sole need of a Savior because we are powerless to save our selves. This is actually the spirit of antichrist that John was talking about in 1 John. Scary.

Notice I didn't lump all Messianic Believers into this category like the authors of these anti-grace books do with the Grace Movement. That is what I called earlier "Scandalous Exposé Christian Media". Those who do that are no better some of the biased media venues out there today who don't really care about truth; only that they appear to be right. SELAH. (Take a minute and breathe.)

Job and His Insolence

I just painted the perfect picture of the person we have been studying. Job thought that by his actions he could justify himself. He declared his righteousness to be more than God's. Isn't that something? He spoke contemptibly and rudely towards God in thinking that he himself had something to do with making himself righteous.

He declares later that he had no clue who God was or what He was like. Isn't that something? Right after that, God gives him double of what he had before. NOW I AM READY TO TELL YOU HOW TO OVERCOME HABITUAL CRISIS IN YOUR LIFE!

What I haven't told you about myself is that I, in the past, had a reoccurring issue in my life. It is the reason that God had me write this book. This book, originally, was meant to change ME. My reoccurring issue has been Habitual Crisis.

What do I mean by Habitual Crisis? I have had so many start overs in my life because I would find myself in a bad situation that I could not overcome. I would then have to start over. This didn't always happen. I realized recently that it started right after a pivotal point in my life.

Remember the story I shared where I was asking God to be real to me and then He said to me, "You first"? He was challenging me to be honest with myself and Him. That was a good thing. . . at first. Before I get into that, I want to talk about an epidemic in the Grace Movement. I have noticed a pattern in many people in the Grace Movement. They preach radical grace and what they have to say is awesome. The only problem is that the evidence to back it up in their lives is not visible. I know one man that used to be my pastor who helped to lay the foundation of Grace in my life. His messages were so radically impacting in my life and are still influencing me to this day. BUT, this man is now bound to a wheelchair with horribly racking back pain and can no longer pastor. This is just one of many examples I could give you. He shares one thing in common with me and with others who practiced but didn't see the fruit.

My Last Restart

Recently I moved, by the direction of the Holy Spirit through dreams, prayer and prophetic direction, to the area of Minneapolis Minnesota. I didn't want to move AGAIN. I didn't have it in me to move again. I had moved and started over so many times it was sickening. It was one of the biggest reasons that my wife divorced me. She was sick of restarting. This last restart, though, was actually brought on by the Holy Spirit. So, I find myself in an unfamiliar land with the same problems of financial insecurity, obscurity, etc. Here we go again. Only this time, God had brought me to a point where He was going to surprise me with a Paradigm Shift. You see, every single failure in my life in the past 13 or 14 years had a certain stamp on it. I would get to a certain point where the "spiritual and mental rubber band" had been stretched to the limit. In that heightened moment I would make a terrible choice. I would do what Job did. I would start throwing accusations at God and blasting Him for not taking care of me. I would yell and scream and fuss at Him for not doing for me what He does for everyone else. I would vent until I was empty. I then would experience a feeling of relief where it would seem that He was starting to move on my behalf. I thought that I did the right thing by being honest with God about my feelings, but what I was really doing was sabotaging myself. I took what He told me to do back then as a something He wanted me to do permanently. I also thought, "Well, I am in right fellowship with Him now because of Grace, so this is ok." That, I found out later, had been my downfall.

Recently I found myself coming to that point again. I moved here and was unable to find a well paying job. I was behind on rent. I had no money, no food and I was running out of gas long before payday. During this time, God started speaking to me about something that appeared random to me. I kept seeing, playing in my head, scenes from movies where government agents were in a test run trying to disarm a time bomb. The pressure was mounting and right at the last second they would cut the blue wire. There was a simulated explosion and a buzzer noise that announced that they had failed to disarm the bomb. The pressure that was there in that moment was now gone, even though they cut the wrong wire. They were then told that they had to do another test run to dismantle another bomb.

I found myself contemplating telling God how I felt when God spoke clearly to me, "Don't cut the wrong wire."

He said it many times. He then revealed to me what He meant. My situations were to be compared to the government agent trying to

170

diffuse the bomb. They were in the heat of the moment and cut the wrong wire. The relief of pressure was not from dismantling the bomb, but from the failure of the test from cutting the wrong wire. "Don't cut the wrong wire." It finally hit me. I was now determined that when that heated time of 1 second before the bomb went off, I was not going to cut the wrong wire.

So, there I was, in the church parking lot on Mother's Day. I got in my car after church. My emotions were already heightened because of Mother's Day without a mother. I sat in my car looking at an empty tank with no money and no food. I was at the 1 second mark of the time bomb. In that moment, instead of doing what I had normally done, which was to blast God for not taking care of me, I began to worship. I began sobbing uncontrollably. I said, "God, You are so good. You have been so good to me. If You don't do another thing for me, You have already done way more than enough with Your sacrifice on the Cross. You are so amazing. I love you so much and I thank You for Your love for me. I can't thank You enough for what You have done. So, in this moment where I feel like I am going to disappear into the night, I declare Your goodness. I declare that You are more than enough for me. I am so thankful. I love You so much!"

It went on and on as the tears streamed down my face. In that moment, all the pain was washed away. It was the purest moment of my life. I was declaring how Awesome He had been to me.I finished it with, "Are You proud of me? Was that good?"

He gave me a resounding "YES!"

The next day, everything changed. The job that I had been working at that seemed to be going nowhere told me that they wanted to train me as a supervisor, that I was their most valued employee, that they were switching me to the shift I wanted and that they were giving me a substantial raise. The church that I thought had been ignoring my resume asked me to come in for an interview for a job. The blog that no one was reading was now getting 100 hits a day. A big named person in the Christian Broadcasting Industry called my cell phone out of the blue to give me pointers. WHAT?

EVERYTHING BEGAN CHANGING, but it started with me giving God my emotions in the heat of my situation. I changed my confession when it really mattered. Not just in everyday confession. Not just in passing, but when the time bomb was about to go off and I was about to lose everything. THAT IS WHEN IT REALLY COUNTS! That is when you know that what you are saying, you truly believe.

I can't put it any plainer than that. I am going to end with that. Sure, I could go on and give you scripture references, but I think you get the point. It takes that 1 second moment to see what you really believe. And in that moment, if you are not declaring the Goodness of God that you normally declare in the ho-hum moments of your life, then you don't really believe it.

I didn't worship God in that moment to get out of my situation. I really thought I was perishing. I worshiped Him because I thought that He was good, Period. And just as Shadrach, Meshach and Abednego saw the son of God in the flames of their fiery furnace, and were saved by His Grace when they put God first, regardless of what the outcome was going to be, when you embrace Jesus Christ and His wonder gift of radical, super-abounding grace, and put Him first, then you too will find His Grace in the Flames!

Chapter 16: *Conclusion*

I pray that the message in this book is branded on your heart and creates a paradigm shift in you that will change and revolutionize your faith. Once you settle in your heart that God is one hundred percent good, it will open up a door of intimacy with you and the Father like you've never known. Thank you for going on this journey with me.

This concludes our second look at the book of Job. I will end with a Psalm of David that is truly the message of this book.

Psalm 103 (HCSB) *"My soul, praise the Lord, and all that is within me, praise His holy name. My soul, praise the Lord, and do not forget all His benefits."*

"He forgives all your sin; He heals all your diseases. He redeems your life from the Pit; He crowns you with faithful love and compassion. He satisfies you with goodness; your youth is renewed like the eagle."

"The Lord executes acts of righteousness and justice for all the oppressed. He revealed His ways to Moses, His deeds to the people of Israel. The Lord is compassionate and gracious; slow to anger and full of faithful love. He will not always accuse us or be angry forever. He has not dealt with us as our sins deserve or repaid us according to our offenses."

"For as high as the heavens are above the earth, so great is His faithful love toward those who fear Him. As far as the east is from the west, so far has He removed our transgressions from us. As a father has compassion on his children, so the Lord has compassion on those who fear Him. For He

knows what we are made of, remembering that we are dust."

"As for man, his days are like grass – he blooms like a flower of the field; when the wind passes over it, it vanishes, and its place is no longer known. But from eternity to eternity the Lord's faithful love is toward those who fear Him, and His righteousness toward the grandchildren of those who keep His covenant, who remember to observe His instructions. The Lord has established His throne in heaven, and His kingdom rules over all."

"Praise the Lord, all His angels of great strength, who do His word, obedient to His command. Praise the Lord, all His armies, His servants who do His will. Praise the Lord, all His works in all the places where He rules. My soul, praise the Lord!"

Made in the USA
Monee, IL
06 February 2022

90729933R00111